NEUROMA

Selling to the reptilian brain

ENGLISH EDITION

Jonathan Benito Sipos

"Few people see what we are, but everyone sees what we look like."
Machiavelli

"The heart has reasons that reason does not know."
Blaise Pascal (1623-1662)

ABOUT THE AUTHOR. WHO IS JONATHAN BENITO SIPOS?

Jonathan is a professor and researcher of Neuroscience at the Autonomous University of Madrid. At the university, he graduated in Biological Sciences and earned a doctorate in the field of Cellular Biology and Genetics, receiving the Outstanding Cum Laude distinction and the Extraordinary Doctorate Award. He has combined his teaching and research work with various administrative positions, including Director of the Center for Continuing Education, Vice Dean, and Deputy Vice Chancellor for Innovation. At the university, he leads a Neuroscience group whose research findings have been published in prestigious international journals such as Nature, Plos Biology, and eLife.

Due to his extensive teaching experience, he is also sought after as a speaker on Neuroscience. This has led to collaborations with companies such as JOHNSON & JOHNSON, AMERICAN EXPRESS, IBM, HEWLETT-PACKARD, MSD, MERCEDES-BENZ, GLAXOSMITHKLINE, LILLY LABORATORIES, MEDTRONIC, BOSTON SCIENTIFIC, and MANGO.

@_jonathanbenito

INTRODUCTION: Applying Neuroscience to Marketing and Sales opens up an entirely new world for us.

Dear reader, welcome to this book on Neurosales and Neuromarketing. I am firmly convinced that this book will have a profound impact on your perception of the world in general, and specifically on the fields of Sales and Marketing.

I assume that you are already aware of the significance of sales in today's world; otherwise, you probably wouldn't be reading this. However, in case you happen to be one of the few individuals who believe that sales are solely the domain of sales departments, merchants, or charlatans, let me share something with you: if you consider sales as irrelevant to your life, regardless of the nature of your activities, I must warn you that things may not go well for you. Sales permeate every aspect of life. They are unquestionably crucial for professionals whose livelihood depends on directly selling products or services. However, they are equally essential for the female engineer who seeks a raise, the recently divorced man looking for a partner, or the recent master's graduate searching for employment... the list goes on indefinitely. Selling oneself or a product is an inherent part of life. Remember this: without the ability to sell, you will struggle in life. Few people genuinely enjoy the process of selling because it entails risks, stepping out of our comfort zones, and the possibility of failure. However, the disparity between knowing how to sell and not knowing how to sell is the difference between mediocrity and spectacular success in life.

Now, how many of us have been taught the art of selling? Practically none. And when some instruction has been provided, it has often been incomplete or misguided at best. I am not against traditional Marketing and Sales; far from it. However, in order to thrive, they must incorporate scientific principles. They are compelled to recognize the fundamental principle that we will extensively explore in this book: you only make a sale when your client's brain decides to buy from you. This may sound trivial, but it is far from it. You will only achieve success in a sale when something in your customer's brain triggers the decision to purchase your product or service. And what influences the response of your client's brain? That is precisely what this book aims to uncover.

Knowing how to sell, whether it's a product, service, or the value of oneself, is essential in many everyday situations.

In a nutshell, it was previously believed that decisions, including purchase decisions, were rational and based on logical thinking. Consequently, sellers would make rational arguments to highlight the benefits of their products. However, Neuroscience has unequivocally demonstrated that the vast majority (and I emphasize, the immense majority) of decisions we make, including purchasing decisions, are irrational. They stem from subconscious mechanisms [1]. You might wonder, "How is that possible? Are you saying that Homo sapiens sapiens makes most decisions irrationally, like a monkey would?" Well, yes, that is precisely what I'm telling you, and I will illustrate it throughout this book. Whether you believe it or not, science supports this claim— modern, rigorous, and well-established science. Every concept explained in this book has been published in esteemed scientific journals, subjected to rigorous empirical testing. That's why you'll find numerous references throughout the book, to demonstrate that they are not mere inventions of a charlatan. Just as there are individuals who persist in denying the existence of gravity or promoting the idea of a flat Earth, there are also pockets of people who oppose vaccines that protect us from once-devastating viruses. You are free to make your own decisions, but if you genuinely want to enhance your sales skills, you must embrace the path of Science, or else remain stagnant where you are.

During a purchasing process, an internal battle unfolds between different brain structures, some of which advocate for the purchase, while others resist it (Bossaerts, 2007). This battle is influenced by multiple factors that we are continually unraveling. Do you want to learn about them? Do you desire to exponentially increase your sales capabilities? Well, then hop on board, let's embark on this journey together!

[1] *Some authors differentiate between the subconscious and the unconscious. However, for the sake of pragmatism in this book, we will use both terms interchangeably to encompass everything that lies beneath the threshold of consciousness.*

BIOLOGICAL BASIS OF BEHAVIOR AND DECISION-MAKING

How does the brain make decisions? The scientific foundations of Neuromarketing and Neurosales

SUBCONSCIOUS DECISION-MAKING WITH RATIONAL ARGUMENTS: HOW DOES THE BRAIN MAKE DECISIONS?

One of the most surprising discoveries for neuroscientists in recent years has been that the vast majority of decisions made by human beings are irrational. These decisions are made unconsciously, even though we try to justify them rationally. It is remarkable how the brain is adept at providing us with rational justifications for events of which it itself is not aware. To illustrate this, consider the example of individuals who undergo a commissurotomy, a surgery in which the corpus callosum, the structure connecting the two cerebral hemispheres, is removed. In this "split brain" condition, the hemispheres are unable to communicate with each other. In experiments, information and questions are presented exclusively to one hemisphere, while the other hemisphere remains unaware of the information received. Surprisingly, when the hemisphere that was not exposed to the information is asked to explain the decision made by its partner hemisphere, it offers rational justifications, despite having no knowledge of the information. This demonstrates our remarkable ability to make sense of things, even when we lack information.

This may initially be hard to believe, as it contradicts our perception of being in control of the choices we make. We often feel that we consciously decide based on weighing pros and cons. However, as we will explore throughout this book, the brain makes decisions based on subconscious mechanisms rooted in ancient and primitive logic. Understanding the logic of the brain is crucial.

The reality is that in the majority of cases when the brain is confronted with a decision, it is the subconscious mechanisms that decide, while the conscious part of the brain subsequently attempts to rationalize and justify the decision to us or to anyone who questions it. As we delve into the book, we will discover that these subconscious processes are heavily influenced, if not entirely driven, by emotions. One could even refer to them as emotional decisions. Our senses provide us with information about the environment, and the processing of this information triggers emotions that largely dictate the decisions we make. This means that decisions can be influenced through sensory input. It doesn't sound bad, does it?

Essentially, all subconscious processes culminate in a battle between two brain structures, with the victorious structure determining the verdict of "I buy" or "I don't buy." In the case of everyday non-reflective purchases (reflective ones would be buying a car, a house, or a computer), this decision process takes approximately 2.5 seconds. For reflective purchases, this battle can extend over weeks. The two structures involved are the brain's reward center and the "loss aversion" center. If the perceived loss aversion outweighs the predicted reward, no purchase will occur; otherwise, a purchase will be made.

For example, consider an extreme case where the loss aversion outweighs the perceived reward: nearly all men would like to own a Ferrari (we will explore in later chapters the biological factors that drive this desire). However, very few can afford to buy a Ferrari, and even among those who can, they may not anticipate enough reward to justify the price and what they have to sacrifice to obtain it. In this scenario, loss aversion triumphs over the reward center, leading to the decision of "DO NOT BUY."

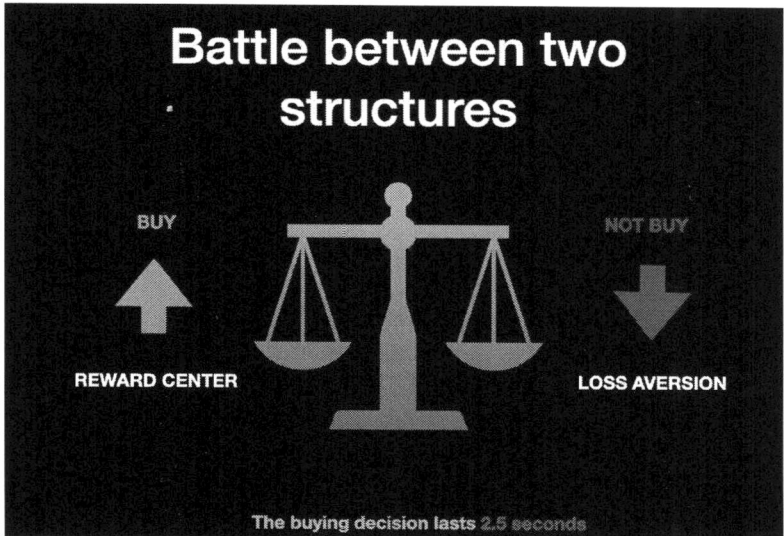

The purchase decision is made in just 2.5 seconds and is the result of a fierce battle between two brain structures: the Reward Center and the Loss Aversion Center.

Then we come across products that are not very expensive, and therefore hardly trigger loss aversion, but they also fail to stimulate the reward center, resulting in the same outcome: "DO NOT BUY." In between, we encounter a wide range of situations where a titanic struggle takes place between the two systems, yielding varying results. It is in this field, where a real battle between the two structures occurs, that we truly have room to maneuver and leverage Neuroscience to tilt the balance in our favor.

It's worth noting that there are indeed pure and strictly rational decisions, but they are quite rare. When a decision is solely based on numbers, and you provide a person with sufficient information and time to decide, the rational aspect takes center stage. However, even in such cases, emotions can still exert their influence. For instance, when purchasing an apartment with identical features, the price will heavily influence the decision. However, subtle emotions triggered by, for example, a captivating view from the apartment's window can sway the decision towards the one that, from a rational standpoint, might be less appealing. It's the classic case of "it has something I like." This dynamic applies to all aspects of decision-making. Sometimes, a business may be financially more promising than another, but we gravitate towards the less lucrative option because it evokes a sense of reward or lacks suspicion (while the one we discard leaves us with the typical and indescribable feeling of "there's something that doesn't quite convince me") that we don't experience with the one we choose.

Furthermore, as mentioned earlier, although

decisions are not rational, we attempt to rationalize everything. We never allow ourselves the luxury of admitting or even contemplating that we are unaware of the reasons behind our decisions. There exists a significant inconsistency between what we believe happens and what truly transpires. We make decisions without precisely knowing why, but when questioned, we provide a plausible rational explanation. That is why we deceive, both others and ourselves. These are not intentional lies, but rather unconscious conspiracies, yet the result is the same: we utter something that isn't true. If asked whether we would buy something, without intending to deceive, it is likely that our response would differ from our actual behavior. Simply put, we think one thing but do another. Consequently, traditional marketing tools such as focus groups and surveys are unreliable. Had the Austrian billionaire Dietrich Mateschitz relied solely on surveys and focus groups, Red Bull would not be among the world's most successful companies today, given that 50% of consumers expressed their lack of interest in the drink. They didn't like it at all. As we will explore later, the Austrian billionaire quickly identified the symbolic value of his product—increased energy—and Red Bull became arguably the first energy drink. Hence, the taste of the product took a backseat; what truly mattered was that its consumption provided a heightened state of energy.

I hope it is now clear to you that the vast majority of decisions are unconscious. What are the interests of the subconscious? How can we win it over? That's what the remainder of the book aims to address…

The case of Red Bull serves as a highly illustrative example that focus groups are not always reliable tools for gauging consumers' true purchase intentions. In 1984, surveys and focus groups were conducted, and 50% of the participants expressed that the product was not appealing in the slightest. Nevertheless, Dietrich Mateschitz made a bold decision to invest heavily in it.

THE THEORY OF THE THREE BRAINS

The theory was proposed in 1970 by the American neuroscientist MacLean. From the perspective of contemporary neuroscience, this theory is somewhat outdated and requires further clarifications. However, it still serves as an excellent model for laypeople to comprehend the functioning of the brain in the specific context that concerns us.

THE THEORY OF THE THREE BRAINS

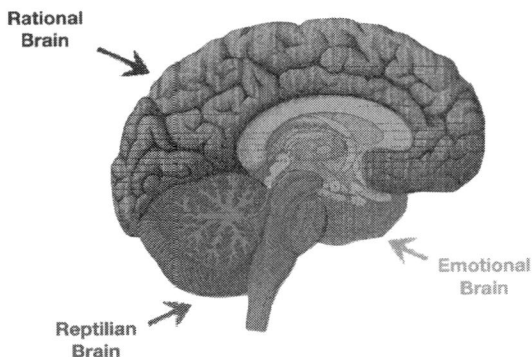

Rational Brain

Emotional Brain

Reptilian Brain

MacLean 1970

I understand that at this point, every reader will recall, in some way, the theory of evolution proposed by Charles Darwin in 1859 (Darwin 1859). In a nutshell, we can say that all living beings originate from the simplest forms that have inhabited and continue to inhabit the planet: unicellular organisms. Some of these beings have evolved and gained complexity, passing through various life forms, with notable milestones including sponges, jellyfish, various types of worms, arthropods, fish, amphibians, reptiles, birds, and finally mammals. The complexity also increases within mammals, eventually leading to primates and culminating in humans. Throughout this evolutionary process, the nervous systems of these animals have become increasingly complex.

Therefore, our brain represents a sophistication of the most primitive forms, and one can argue that modules have been added over the course of evolution. The modules that function effectively are retained, while new ones are added to perform additional tasks. From this perspective, it is practical to assume that the human brain consists of three major modules, blocks, or, as they were called in the past, "brains": the reptilian brain (also known as the old brain), the emotional brain (also known as the limbic system), and the modern brain (also known as the rational or neocortex).

The most primitive brain is known as the reptilian brain or the old brain. Figuratively speaking, this is the brain that makes decisions. Which decisions, you may ask? Well, we could say all of them, as it has the final say even without our conscious awareness. Its primary focus, as we will explore in detail, is centered around survival and reproduction. It is directly responsible for the perpetuation of our genes and remains anchored in the ancestral world, particularly in matters directly related to these two functions (survival and reproduction). It does not possess emotions or reasoning abilities and exists in the present moment. Of course, when making decisions, it often relies on information received from the other two brains: primarily the emotional brain and, as mentioned before, the rational brain in specific circumstances, particularly when sufficient time is available. Therefore, it is crucial to understand the ancestral logic of this brain in order to connect with it, understand how to convey messages that resonate with it, and ultimately, to be able to sell effectively.

We share the reptilian brain with animals much older than us, hence its name, derived from reptiles. It is the cradle of survival and reproduction, and thanks to its decisions, you and I exist.

The emotional brain is fascinating, and we share it with other mammals. You can tell when your dog is sad, just as your dog knows when you are sad. It is evident that this information is communicated through non-verbal language, and we comprehend it in an instinctive and irrational manner. The emotional system has a significant impact on the reptilian brain and greatly influences its decision-making, more than we realize.

The emotional brain is what allows us to perceive that the dog on the left is happy, while the one at the bottom is sad. And, of course, they can also discern our mood.

The rational brain, or neocortex, is the inheritance of highly evolved animals, and we can affirm that it is sufficiently developed in primates and fully developed in humans. This neocortex grants us various abilities, including rationality. It is where conscious thoughts are generated. We often assume that it is this rational brain that is in control, but the reality is quite different. Quantifying it precisely is challenging, but scientific estimates suggest that 95% of mental processes occur outside of consciousness (Zaltman 2004). Interestingly, it is the only one of the three brains that possesses language abilities. When you ask a customer about their product experience or their potential purchase, the information they provide is rational. To understand the experiences of the other two brains, we need to employ modern neuroscience techniques, which we will explore in this book.

Historically, the majority of sales strategies have focused on a rational approach targeting the modern brain, the neocortex. However, these strategies are often ineffective. If you genuinely wish to succeed in sales—and in life as a whole—you have no choice but to abandon outdated strategies and misconceptions, and learn how to sell to the subconscious, which, as we have seen, holds the ultimate decision-making power.

Remember: Instinct takes precedence over emotion, and emotion prevails over logic.

We share the rational brain with primates.

BIBLIOGRAPHY

Bossaerts, BK a. P. (2007). "Neural Antecedents of Financial Decisions." The Journal of Neuroscience **27** ((31)): 8174-8177.

Lindstrom, M. (2012). Buyology. Truths And Lies Of Why We Buy - 1st Edition , Booket. Divulgation. Present.

Zaltman, G. (2004). How consumers think

THE BIOLOGICAL CODE IN NEUROSALES

What was our brain designed for? The biological code.

I magine that you design a machine to perform a specific function within a well-defined context. You excel at robotics and create exceptional machines. This particular machine you've built is programmed to generate millions of precise and refined outputs, which vary based on the range of inputs it receives. When a stimulus is received, it processes it and produces an accurate response. It's a marvel. Now, consider that this machine falls into the hands of someone who doesn't understand its purpose or how it was designed, nor the context in which it was created. They start using your machine for purposes other than its intended function. Your machine performs these tasks proficiently, but the potential results would be immense if they understood its original purpose and context.

Something similar happens with our brain. It was designed, let's say through evolution (we won't delve into that in this book), to produce specific outputs from certain inputs in a specific scenario. By the way, this scenario is far from sitting in front of a computer screen deciding whether or not to click and buy the latest iPhone model.

Therefore, for any sales professional, trader, or even individuals aiming for success and fewer problems in life, it's crucial to know how to communicate with the brains of those around us. Understanding how this remarkable machine works is vital. To achieve this, we must inevitably comprehend the context in which it was designed and its intended purpose. By doing so, we can obtain better results for everyone. Do you find this interesting? Well, let's delve into it!

I won't delve deeply into the theoretical framework of Biology behind all this, but you should know some essential ideas to fully comprehend the decisions our brain makes when purchasing or rejecting a product, or any other decision for that matter. In some chapters, it may appear categorical or even blunt to those unfamiliar with Biology and Neuroscience. However, trust me, I'm not expressing my opinions but rather synthesizing thousands of scientific publications that support these theories.

There's a concept that is well-developed in a classic book on Biology called "The Selfish Gene: The Biological Bases of Our Behavior" by Richard Dawkins. Its first version was released in 1976, and it has been continually updated (Dawkins, 2014). The concept Richard elaborates on is that, essentially, we are vessels of genes—selfish genes that have developed sophisticated strategies to perpetuate themselves. Remember, our genes are selfish, and their sole interest is their own perpetuation. They couldn't care less about the perpetuation of our neighbor's genes. In fact, they prefer that the neighbor's genes don't survive as they directly compete with their own interests. And what does this have to do with sales and neuromarketing? It's a legitimate question... Well, you need to see the big picture, my dear friend... EVERYTHING.

From my perspective, and the more we advance in our research, the more Richard's summary of the interests and strategies of genes resonates with me. Species strive to survive and reproduce, and within a species, each individual competes against others to ensure their own perpetuation, the perpetuation of their genes. Consequently, a multitude of neural mechanisms work to ensure that you and I reproduce, fight, and even die if necessary, all to guarantee the reproduction of our offspring... and when taken to the extreme, these mechanisms ensure that this occurs with the utmost precision.

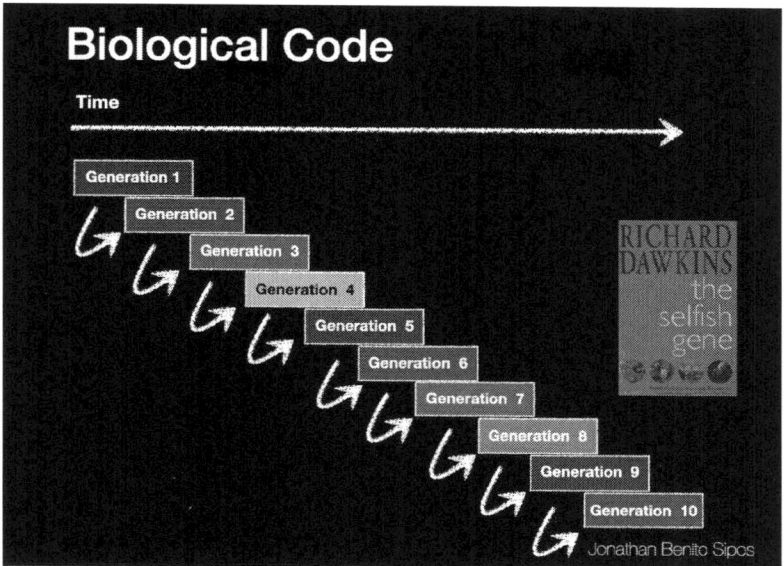

According to the theories of Richard Dawkins, we are vessels of genes whose primary concern is to reproduce and live long enough to care for our offspring until they are capable of reproducing themselves.

In different species, individuals, typically males in this case, engage in fights to have the opportunity to select a female mate (we will explore later what this signifies from a biological perspective and its relevance to marketing). This internal program is observed across arthropods and primates alike.

Our brain has evolved to ensure survival and reproduction in a vastly different context from our current way of life. Various brain mechanisms are involved in survival, while others are dedicated to reproduction. In the case of human beings, who are inherently social creatures, we have a programmed set of behaviors related to our interactions within a "pack." I hope it doesn't offend you, but not too long ago, we lived in primitive herds, specifically in trees. It's crucial to grasp this concept because, for instance, it explains why we have an innate, DNA-encoded fear of spiders and snakes. These creatures were among our greatest threats when we lived in trees, and this genetic memory, incredible as it may seem, persists. As I mentioned, our life within the pack has conditioned us in unexpected ways, as rejection from the pack could mean the inability to reproduce and, consequently, death (solitary individuals struggle with hunting). Understanding these mechanisms is essential for comprehending many of the experiences we encounter today. It may seem distant, but knowing their logic is crucial if we wish to understand how we make decisions—both in purchasing and in other aspects of human life. Therefore, if you want to learn how to sell, you must understand life in a herd. Let's gradually delve into it!

The herd, the group, has been with us for millions of years. Many of our present behaviors are linked to this concept of the group.

BIOLOGY IN MARKETING AND SALES

J urgen Klaric, one of the worldwide Marketing gurus, asserts that "you can learn to sell more by reading Biology than Marketing" (Klaric 2017). It is becoming increasingly evident that modern Marketing cannot progress without understanding the fundamental principles of Biology, including Behavioral Biology, Physiology, Genetics, and Psychology.

Regardless of our culture, upbringing, and environment, all human beings are remarkably similar, if not identical, at a fundamental level. As we have previously seen, the basis of our decisions remains the same: we are intricately programmed machines with primal instincts aimed at survival and reproduction. Those who fail to comprehend the basic mechanisms of Biology will encounter significant challenges in business and various aspects of life.

I understand that individuals outside the realm of Biology may be skeptical of these approaches. They might argue that rationality sets us apart from animals, implying that our decisions are distinguished by our intellect. While it is true that our values allow us to partially override our instincts, it is important to recognize that a Wall Street broker does not base their decision to buy or sell currencies solely on rationality. In a later chapter, we will delve into the mechanisms by which the brain makes decisions. However, before that, let me share with you an experiment conducted with capuchin monkeys as a mere illustration of our animalistic nature when making decisions in the marketplace.

Capuchin monkey (*Cebus apella*)

In 2005, a group led by neuroscientist Laurie Santos from Yale University trained seven capuchin monkeys (Cebus apella) in the concepts of money management and value (Chen and Santos, 2006). Capuchins are primarily driven by the desire for food and sex. The researchers selected a silver disk with a hole in the center as a representation of their currency, and the capuchins learned that they could exchange this coin for fruit. Each monkey was given twelve coins, and different fruits were assigned varying prices to analyze their spending decisions. The researchers observed that the capuchins exhibited remarkable budget management skills. When the researchers manipulated the prices of the fruits, the monkeys responded in a manner consistent with the principles of human economics. Furthermore, when the monkeys were taught to gamble, they made similar irrational decisions to those of human gamblers. The data extracted from capuchin monkeys shows that their buying behavior is statistically similar to that of many present-day stock investors. In summary, it can be said that the purchasing behavior of monkeys is not significantly different from that of human beings.

Therefore, dear friend, do not underestimate the biological code. There is increasing evidence that the decisions we make are influenced by deep-seated ancestral programming that is challenging to override. Understanding this programming better will benefit you greatly.

BIOLOGICAL STATUS CODE.

I f you realize, human beings in general allocate many resources (temporary, monetary, energetic, sentimental) to acquire a certain status, a relevant position within the group. It is true that there are individuals in particular who presume to avoid that status, but it is not common. Unless this feeling is true and genuine, almost all of them -sometimes even unconsciously- fight not to be excluded from a group and to not occupy the most disadvantageous positions within it.

Why do we have such an ingrained program aimed at that end? As you will see, I am going to explain a series of biological mechanisms that justify the existence of the mental programs that we possess. My goal with this is for you to understand the interests of our brain well because only in this way will you be able to understand consumer behaviors. It is true that, as always, values and culture can mitigate these instincts, but they do not always succeed. These instincts try to escape at the slightest opportunity, and if you are not convinced, think about why people continue buying brands or looking for good but cheap imitations. No, it's no coincidence. Biology breaks in as soon as it can.

Okay, so what does gaining status mean biologically?

Well, it is neither more nor less than climbing hierarchical positions in "the pack". And why are we so interested in positioning ourselves at the top of that hierarchy? What is behind that lust for power? The explanation responds to a deep and ancestral, but simple biological code. Occupying privileged positions in the pack hierarchy means:

1. Having a much better chance of survival because it implies advantageous access to resources (for example, food), and that extends to both you and your progeny. Preferential access to resources is a very powerful argument for your reptilian brain. By positioning yourself at the top, you can offer your progeny extra protection, and the chances, therefore, that your genes will be perpetuated are much higher. Remember that this is the deep obsession of your brain: the perpetuation of your genes.

2. The second big advantage of being high up in the pack hierarchy is that you have a much better chance of choosing a mate, regardless of gender. Having more possibilities to choose makes it easier to select a beautiful partner, and that is not trivial. We don't like beautiful people by chance. Beautiful people tend to be people who have high symmetry because we have a mental program (heuristic shortcut) that tells us that symmetrical people have more chances of developing good health. And this heuristic shortcut is not without reason. For years, in our research group, we have had open lines of study of Developmental Neurobiology. Generating symmetry is not easy. Hundreds and

hundreds of genes orchestrated with exquisite regulation participate in the creation of this symmetry. The slightest mistake makes the symmetry go haywire. Therefore, if a good facial symmetry is shown (as I say, nothing easy to achieve from the point of view of Developmental Biology), it is very likely that the "genetic machinery" of the bearer of the symmetry works better than that of an individual whose face does not have facial symmetry. And a good functioning of said machinery implies a lower probability of diseases, having children with a greater possibility of being symmetrical, and therefore with a greater potential to be healthy and find a partner... the whiting that bites its own tail.

Then there is something very important, which I will try to explain in a simple way. Everything is based on a biological concept called anisogamy, which means that the gametes of the male and the female are not the same. And what does this have to do with consumer behavior? Understanding this is understanding so many things that happen in life. I'm going to argue. What follows is the Biology of all the species that suffer from

Symmetrical people are very attractive. The brain interprets that external symmetry implies better genetic *fitness,* and Developmental Biology convincingly agrees

A man has at his disposal millions and millions of gametes every day, so in an optimistic scenario, the man could literally have thousands of children. That is to say, the possibilities of perpetuation of women's genes depend on the future of 36 descendants, while that of men depends on the future of hundreds or thousands of them. The difference is not trivial, far from it. Remember that the number one objective of our biological code is for our genes to be perpetuated, and it is clear that women have a very disadvantageous situation in this regard, so they must be extremely demanding when choosing the man with whom to have children, to maximize the chances of their survival. The woman's brain is not going to allow her egg to be fertilized by the first one that passes by, for this reason, women are very selective when it comes to finding a partner. What does it mean to be selective? Fundamentally, it means that she has to find a man who guarantees her good genes, as well as protection and care for her progeny. It's the least she deserves, and not all men are going to guarantee it. The last thing a woman wants is to waste one of those valuable gametes that nature has given her, so she will flee from that man who does not offer her a minimum of guarantees when it comes to raising his progeny.

On the contrary, the man can allow himself the luxury of being very little selective because he has the possibility of "playing more times in the evolutionary lottery", but he obviously shows an insulting preference for having his children with the most beautiful (most symmetrical) woman, larger breasts (a heuristic shortcut by which he interprets that his children will not lack milk), etc. Therefore, the man will fight to the death (literally, at least in feral nature) to position himself at the top of the hierarchy and thus be able to choose the best possible partner. Because let's not fool ourselves... the choice of a partner, both for men and women, does not stop responding to the laws of supply and demand, and it does not stop being one of the most important choices (of "buying" with all the love and quotes, not to be taken out of context) of our life. I insist, all these behaviors are unconscious; no one goes through life saying, "What a symmetrical man, if I have children with him, it is probable that they will not develop diseases..." No, they are subconscious mental routines, but don't forget that they are what do they send.

And what does all this have to do with markets? Well, this has to do with EVERYTHING because by understanding what I have just explained, you will understand the true instincts of the human being, and therefore the needs that arise from these instincts. Culture, education, and rationality, obviously, can hide these instincts, but remember that they will try to come out at all costs, just like when you are on a diet and you are hungry, you can control eating vs. not eating, but the brain will be there for you, "kindly" urging them to eat because it is part of their internal program, it is their way of telling you, "be careful, if you don't eat, we can die."

In short, never underestimate the desire for status, recognition, and power that most human beings have. It is not for nothing that we will see that many of the services and products are exclusively designed to increase status (Veblen products that we will see later), and you will discover that human beings are capable of making great sacrifices to obtain these products and services.

BIBLIOGRAPHY

Chen MK, LV, Santos LR. (2006). "How basic are behavioral biases? Evidence from capuchin monkey trading behavior. ." J Polit Econ. **114** : 517–537. .

DAWKINS, R. (2014). THE SELFISH GENE: THE BIOLOGICAL BASE OF OUR BEHAVIOR , SALVAT EDITORES SA.

Klaric, J. (2017). Sell to the mind, not to the people Paidós Empresa.

THE NEURAL BATTLE BEFORE A PURCHASING DECISION: THE BRAIN'S REWARD CENTER AND THE LOSS AVERSION CENTER.

THE BRAIN'S REWARD CENTER: PURCHASE MODE ON.

A s we have mentioned before, the purchase decision is primarily influenced by the interplay between two systems: the reward system and the loss aversion system. The activation of the reward center motivates us to make purchases, while the activation of the loss aversion system urges us to hold onto our money (Bossaerts 2007). Let's now explore the reward system in more detail.

The reward center is a complex structure both in terms of its anatomy and neurophysiology. It does not reside in a single, well-defined location but rather operates through intricate processes. To simplify things (quite a bit), we can say that it is primarily located in a structure called the Nucleus Accumbens, and the key neurotransmitter involved in these processes is dopamine. The reward center is activated whenever we perform or anticipate actions that are beneficial to us as individuals and as a species. For instance, it is triggered when we drink (especially when we are thirsty, think about the pleasure you felt the last time you quenched your thirst with water), eat (especially when hungry), engage in sexual activity, urinate or defecate, acquire something that enhances our status, and so on. In essence, it is activated by actions that promote survival and reproduction. This phenomenon is observed not only in humans but also in other mammals (and likely throughout the animal kingdom).

The The Brain Reward Center is activated during acts that are essential for survival and/or reproduction. It is evolution's strategy to motivate us to engage in these behaviors by rewarding us for performing them and punishing us for neglecting them.

Thanks to the activation of the brain reward system, we find motivation to perform the actions described above. Its activation can also induce optimism and, at times, overconfidence, leading us to take unnecessary risks. It's worth noting that there are Neuromarketing techniques that aim to stimulate the reward center, as we will explore later. Conversely, when the activation of this reward system is low, known as hypoactivation, individuals may experience a lack of energy, fatigue, and apathy. This can trigger a search for actions that stimulate the activation of this system, such as substance abuse, impulsive buying, or gambling.

Drugs of abuse, such as cocaine, primarily increase dopamine levels in these brain structures, resulting in feelings of well-being and overconfidence. Similar rewards can be obtained from certain actions, such as buying something that brings us satisfaction or receiving a gift we like. The manipulation of dopamine levels in these structures can be highly addictive, leading individuals to seek out substances or processes that replicate this effect as frequently as possible. Hence, for some people, the act of buying can become one of the most addictive behaviors.

In subsequent chapters, we will explore practical examples that effectively activate the brain reward center.

Shopping also activates the reward center and can be highly addictive.

LOSS AVERSION. PURCHASE MODE OFF

A s with the reward center, the loss aversion system is not devoid of complexity, both anatomically and neurophysiologically.

To simplify, we will primarily discuss two main structures of the loss aversion center. The first is the amygdala, an almond-shaped nucleus located deep within the temporal lobe. When the amygdala is intentionally stimulated, usually through electric shocks in experiments, it evokes profound feelings of fear, restlessness, and anguish. It is clear that human beings dislike the activation of the amygdala, as the accompanying sensations are far from pleasant, leading us to avoid triggering it at all costs. The second structure is the insula, which responds to pain and potential risks. It has been observed that individuals with insula injuries tend to take greater risks than those without such injuries. Prolonged activation of the loss aversion system leads to stress, anxiety, feelings of disgust, pain, and even panic.

Losing our possessions, especially valuable ones like money, generates significant stress and anxiety. The discomfort caused by losing 300 euros outweighs the reward of winning the same amount. In fact, studies conducted by Daniel Kahneman and Amos Tversky demonstrate that losses are psychologically valued with an intensity 1.5 to 2.5 times greater than gains. This aversion to loss has a profound biological basis, extending beyond humans. An interesting study by Chen et al. involved training capuchin monkeys (Cebus apella) to trade token coins for food with researchers. The monkeys had a choice between two experimenters who provided the same number of apples in each trial but did so in different ways. The "gain experimenter" showed the monkey one apple and occasionally added an extra apple, while the "loss experimenter" started with two apples and sometimes removed one. The monkeys overwhelmingly preferred the gain experimenter over the loss experimenter, despite receiving the same benefit from both. This study demonstrates that deep aversion to loss is not exclusive to humans and is part of an ancient biological program.

Practical tip:

This aversion to loss can be effectively utilized by Neuromarketing in various ways, as we will explore. Here, we will present an example of a fascinating strategy: initiating a negotiation with a product or service that includes all available options, and then providing the consumer with the opportunity to eliminate options one by one to reduce the price of the final product or service. Since the primitive part of the brain dislikes losing out on potential gains, it will always strive to minimize its losses. For instance, when selling a car, it is more astute to offer a fully loaded model and allow the customer to progressively eliminate specific features. The primitive brain will be motivated to lose as little as possible, resulting in the chosen car having a greater number of extras compared to a strategy typically employed by car salespeople, where a basic car is presented and accessories are added incrementally.

"GOGGLE EFFECT" (NOT GOOGLE)

"**G**oggle" in English refers to diving glasses, and this effect suggests that the perception of the world can vary depending on the lenses we use.

As we have discussed throughout this book, the purchase decision is influenced by the interaction between two brain systems: one that favors purchasing (the reward center) and the other that discourages it (loss aversion). Now, the "Goggle Effect" involves introducing a primary stimulus, initially unrelated to the product or service being sold, that activates the reward center (particularly the nucleus accumbens). This activation leans the purchase decision towards a "yes." In essence, it entails intentionally introducing a primary stimulus that unconsciously facilitates the purchase of a secondary product.

What types of primary stimuli are commonly used? Any stimulus that activates the reward center, anything that conveys wealth, success, sex, beauty, food, pleasure... Essentially, anything related to hedonism or that is considered "aspirational," arousing the consumer's ego and making them feel exclusive.

Here are some examples of advertising where the Goggle effect is employed. In each case, a primary stimulus is used to preactivate the brain's reward center and enhance the sale of the product or service. As we can observe, this technique has been utilized for many years.

A particularly intriguing subtype of the "Goggle Effect" is induced by alcohol consumption. Scottish researchers have demonstrated what has already been known in popular culture, namely that under the influence of alcohol (the study was conducted after consuming two pints of beer), the faces of less attractive individuals appear more appealing to us (Jones 2003).

Practical tip: How can you leverage the "Goggle Effect" in your business?
This technique works effectively in Visual Marketing. You

need to incorporate a rewarding image (primary element) followed by your product. In our culture, it is preferable to position the primary element on the left or at the top, as we tend to read from left to right or top to bottom.

BIBLIOGRAPHY

Bossaerts, BK a. P. (2007). "Neural Antecedents of Financial Decisions." The Journal of Neuroscience **27** ((31)): 8174-8177.

Chen MK, LV, Santos LR. (2006). "How basic are behavioral biases? Evidence from capuchin monkey trading behavior. ." J Polit Econ. **114** : 517–537. .

Jones, BT, Jones, BC, Thomas, AP and Piper, J. (2003). "Alcohol consumption increases attractiveness ratings of opposite-sex faces: a possible third route to risky sex." Addiction **98** (8):1069-1075.

ANALYSIS TECHNIQUES USED IN NEUROMARKETING

A s we mention throughout the book, there is a distinction between how individuals believe they will react and how they actually respond in real situations. This applies to surveys, focus groups, and specific scenarios. To accurately analyze a person's true behavior in response to stimuli such as advertisements or new products/services, neuromarketing employs scientific tools that provide empirical and verifiable data.

The brain interprets reality through the senses, triggering a range of emotions that manifest as various physiological responses. Some of these responses are well-known and measurable, while others are still being extensively studied. For instance, the emotion of fear elicits an adrenergic discharge, involving the release of adrenaline by the sympathetic nervous system. This leads to increased blood pressure, rapid heartbeat (tachycardia), dilation of muscles' capillaries (preparing them for potential action), and constriction of skin capillaries (causing a pale complexion). These physiological responses, such as heart rate, blood pressure, temperature, sweating, and hormone levels, can be measured to gain valuable insights into an individual's physiological state.

In certain cases, these physiological indicators may not be as apparent or informative as desired. Therefore, additional tools are utilized to directly examine the decision-making processes in the brain, the "engine room" of choices. While it may be impractical for small businesses to employ specialists who employ these techniques, it is worthwhile to understand that most of the practical advice provided in this book is based on these reliable techniques.

ELECTROENCEPHALO GRAM (EEG) AND MORE MODERN VARIANTS.

I n order to communicate with each other, neurons undergo electrical changes in their membranes that can be measured by an electroencephalogram (EEG). These electrical changes can vary in frequency, and each frequency has been associated with different functional states of the brain (such as fear, alertness, sleep, etc.). In other words, the electroencephalogram records the pattern of brain waves in real time, allowing us to understand cognitive processes in response to certain stimuli, such as advertising. This tool enables relatively easy identification of which parts of an advertisement trigger specific emotions or lack of interest. Additionally, it provides crucial information about whether the brain is excited, bored, attentive, or anxious, allowing the removal of uninteresting parts of an ad.

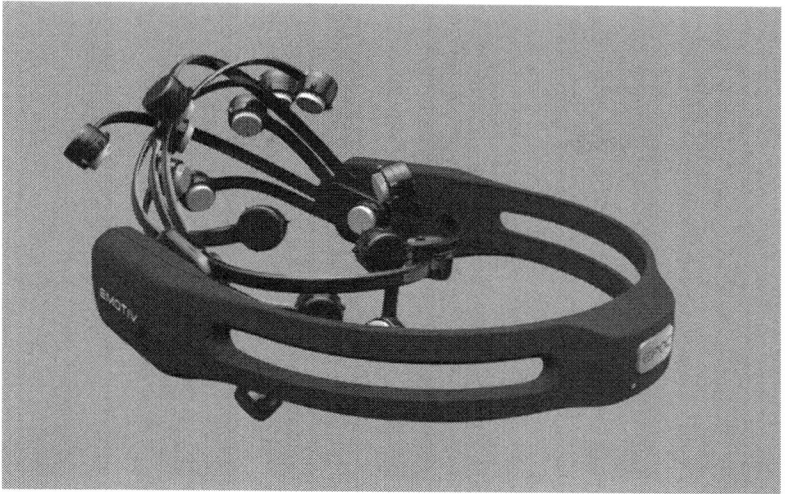

This modern device enables the detection of electrical currents caused by neuronal activity. Unlike older encephalographs, modern devices are much faster to set up, less cumbersome, and also wireless.

ELECTROMYOGRAM AND MORE MODERN VARIANTS

T he contractions of facial muscles provide a wealth of information. Their coordinated contractions can express various emotional states, and the interpretation of this non-verbal language transcends different cultures—it is completely cross-cultural. Some facial muscles, such as the orbicularis oculi, cannot be voluntarily activated, but their contraction is only achieved in specific emotional states.

When a muscle moves, it undergoes an electrical change in its membrane, which can be accurately measured through an electromyogram. For instance, the occipitofrontalis muscle is responsible for raising the eyebrows and wrinkling the forehead, which occurs involuntarily when experiencing feelings of anger. Similarly, the zygomatic muscle is involved in laughter and smiling. While we can consciously try to conceal these responses, the contraction of these muscles is nearly involuntary, and even subtle contractions occur and can be detected.

Duchenne de Boulogne's experiments demonstrated how electrical stimuli-induced contractions can produce facial expressions similar to those naturally caused by emotions.

HIGH-RESOLUTION
IMAGE ANALYSIS

The electromyogram measures the electrical changes that occur in the muscles when they contract, but image analysis goes one step further: it captures contractions that are imperceptible to the naked eye. By analyzing a video captured by a high-resolution camera, we can interpret with great precision the emotions that a specific stimulus has evoked in an individual.

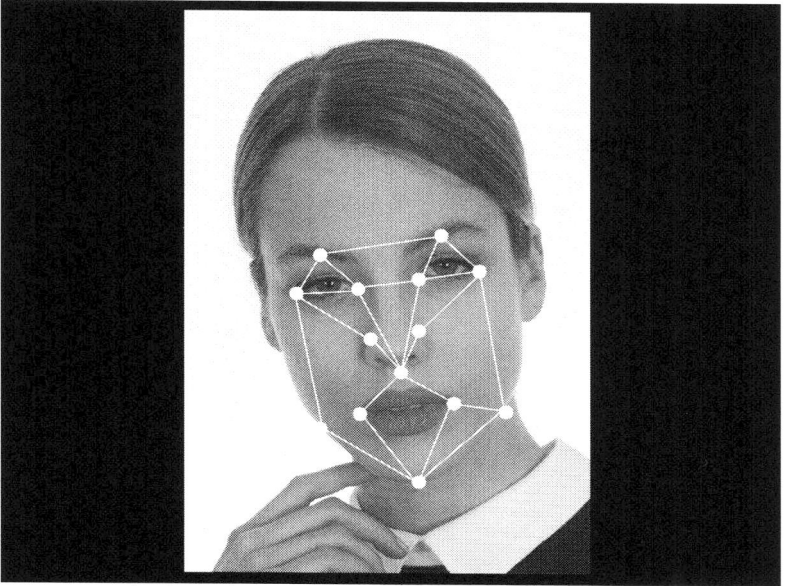

Image analysis techniques use reference points (landmarks) on the face to detect even the slightest movement and interpret the emotions of the study subject.

EYE TRACKING

The direction of our gaze also provides valuable information as it reflects our focus of attention. If we don't look at an object, it indicates that we haven't paid attention to it (unless we intentionally ignore it, but that's a different story). Consequently, it becomes difficult, if not impossible, for that object to be remembered.

Eye tracking systems analyze the precise location where the eyes are directed, allowing us to study the pattern of eye movements and infer the pattern of attention.

Monitoring eye movements has become relatively easy and affordable nowadays, enabling us to gather extensive information about the impact of an object, image, or website on an individual. In this regard, there are numerous advertisements where certain characteristics need to be modified to capture the consumer's attention to the desired data. The figures below depict ads where "eye tracking" experiments reveal that consumers are not focusing on the intended information, but by altering the model's gaze, we significantly alter the consumer's attention.

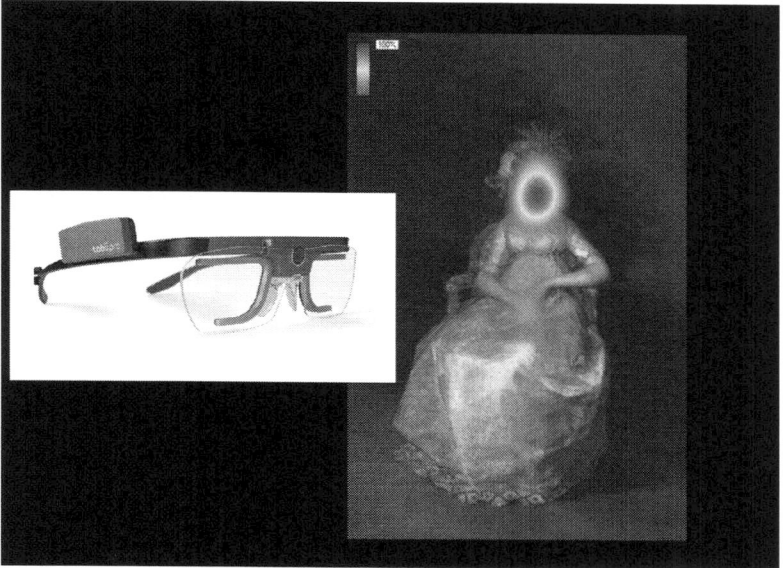

These are the types of glasses used in "Eye Tracking" experiments today. A front-facing camera analyzes the image captured by the eye, while another camera is directed towards the eye camera. This setup allows for precise determination of the exact point at which the wearer of the glasses is looking.

Here we have two examples in which, thanks to eye tracking analysis, it has been possible to modify the advertisements and increase the attention of potential consumers towards the elements we want to highlight (the message and the product). How was this achieved? Simply by changing the gaze of the models, as we naturally tend to follow their gaze. These images are from a study conducted by Neil Patel.

FUNCTIONAL MAGNETIC RESONANCE IMAGING (FMRI)

When a brain region is activated, it requires a greater supply of oxygen compared to when it is not active. This increased oxygen demand is managed by a molecule called hemoglobin, which exhibits different magnetic properties depending on the presence or absence of oxygen in the tissue. As a result, we can monitor the relevant brain regions by using magnetic fields. Magnetic resonance imaging is one of the most impressive techniques as it provides precise information about the active brain regions at any given time. However, one drawback is the high cost associated with this equipment, as they are extremely expensive.

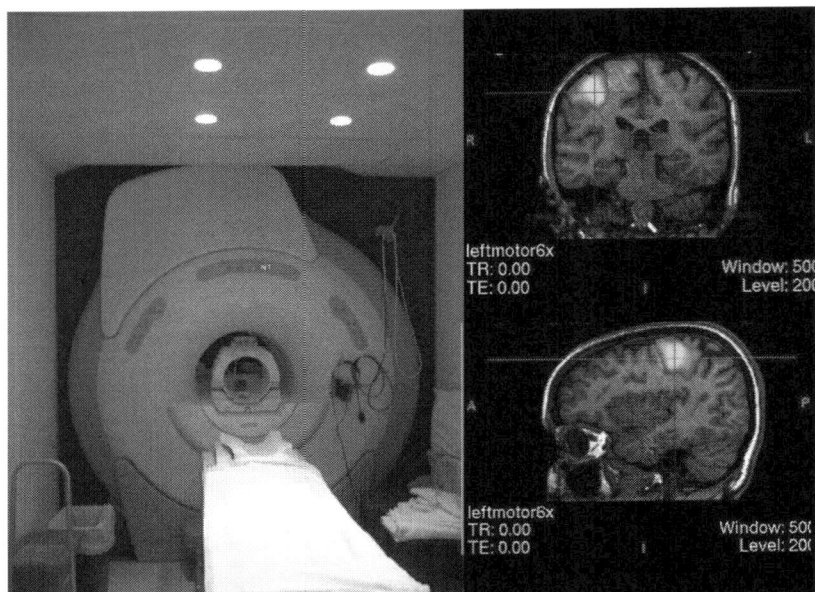

On the left, we can see a modern functional magnetic resonance imaging machine, and on the right, we have the results of the analysis. Thanks to this technique, brain activity can be monitored almost in real time.

HOW TO AROUSE THE INTEREST OF THE REPTILIAN BRAIN? WHAT INTERESTS IT?

HOW TO APPEAL TO THE REPTILIAN BRAIN: COMMUNICATE WITH IT IN ITS OWN LANGUAGE.

N ow that we understand that decisions are not made on a rational level and that in order to succeed in sales, we must directly address the reptilian brain, let's explore what captures its interest and the mechanisms that can help us establish a connection with this ancient ally and make it listen to us.

Whenever you find yourself uncertain or lost in your reasoning, always refer back to the biological code we discussed earlier: What is our biological objective? It is the perpetuation of our DNA, ideally as many times as possible. Remember that from this perspective, we are nothing more than vessels carrying that DNA through generations. Therefore, the reptilian brain, the one responsible for achieving this goal, is the one we need to communicate with. Never underestimate its power; it performs its role exceptionally well and has done so successfully for millions of years, even in hostile environments. Let's get to know this friend we must engage with, so we can strategize and capture its attention and establish effective communication. Let's dive in!

What is the reptilian brain like?

- It is utterly egocentric: it serves as the control center for a vessel carrying genes, and its mission is to ensure the perpetuation of these genes across generations. To achieve this, it primarily focuses on two objectives: survival and reproduction as frequently as possible. Additionally, it must provide utmost attention to its offspring to ensure their survival and successful reproduction. Hence, it can be willing to resort to literal killing if necessary (as any parent would in extreme situations), unless the emotional and rational brain inhibits such behavior. It's essential to recognize that individuals of the same gender are competitors for their genes, as this understanding helps explain certain behaviors. Therefore, it's crucial to grasp that the reptilian brain is highly self-centered and selfish. While its emotional and rational aspects may not be, the reptilian brain certainly is. Consequently, from the outset, your message must offer tangible benefits to capture its attention. Will you solve a problem it has or prevent a potential problem? Will you provide a competitive advantage (e.g., specialized training)? Will you help improve its "status in the pack"? Will you offer rewards that activate its reward center? You must identify the problems others face and provide solutions. We will discuss how to achieve this later.
- It craves contrasts: The reptilian brain doesn't

concern itself with subtle nuances as the emotional and rational brain does, as they are not relevant or essential for immediate survival and fail to capture its attention. In nature, dangers and advantages are discerned through contrasts: big/small, fast/slow, safe/dangerous, bright/dark. Therefore, in your messages, strive to create contrasts between the world of the consumer with your product/service and the world without it. As we will explore later, you can present these contrasts through stories or mini-dramas, which the brain inherently enjoys.

The Windex ad at a bus stop illustrates many important aspects that we will delve into later. In this particular case, let's focus on the concept of contrast. The brain can easily perceive the distinction between using and not using this product.

- You need to anticipate tangible results: It comprehends abstract concepts poorly, so you need to make it straightforward for the reptilian brain. Your product/service should offer advantages that are easily understood: it's the lightest, it's waterproof, it's twice as fast as the competition, it's half as cheap as others...

. Its world is primarily visual: "Not long ago, our survival depended on the ability to navigate a three-dimensional environment where visual perception played a crucial role. The reptilian brain's fast and accurate visual processing allowed us to differentiate between a harmless branch and a deadly snake, determining the difference between life and death. Even today, we remain primarily visual beings. This doesn't mean that our other senses are unimportant—quite the contrary—and we will discuss this in detail later. However, if you want to capture the attention of the reptilian brain, you need to engage it with compelling visual stimuli. We will explore various strategies to achieve this throughout the book."

Our brain is highly visual. It was not long ago when we lived in trees, and our experience of the 3D world was particularly pronounced. The ability to see or not see a snake made all the difference between life and death. The constant struggle between seeing (on our part) and not being seen (on the part of the snake) was a battle for survival.

- The emotional brain has a significant influence on it: As mentioned earlier, while the reptilian brain makes the decisions, the emotional brain plays a crucial role. In the section on memory and learning, we will delve deeper into this point. If you reflect on your own experiences, you'll discover that events with strong emotional components remain deeply ingrained in your memory effortlessly. Therefore, if your message lacks an emotional component, the likelihood of the old brain remembering it diminishes greatly.
- Focus on benefits: It's important to recognize that the old brain doesn't care about the product itself or its features; what matters to it are the benefits it brings. Don't assume that these benefits are self-evident; you need to ensure that the message effectively communicates them. Instead of highlighting your product, service, or company, reverse the message and focus solely on the benefits you'll deliver to the reptilian brain. For example, if you sell air conditioners, emphasize the cool, refreshing air they provide and how they can transform the room's conditions—rather than focusing on the machine itself, which is irrelevant to the old brain. What matters is the impact the air

can have on the brain's environment.

Therefore, your focus should be on showcasing the benefit of your product. Don't worry, I'll make it easy for you. The advantages of your product or service should align with one of the following five categories, which directly concern the reptilian brain. You could consider these categories as the five buttons to activate the interest of the old brain (also referred to as reptilian buttons). To sell your product or service, you need to press at least one of these buttons. If your product or service fits into multiple categories, that's not a problem. Simply identify the main category:

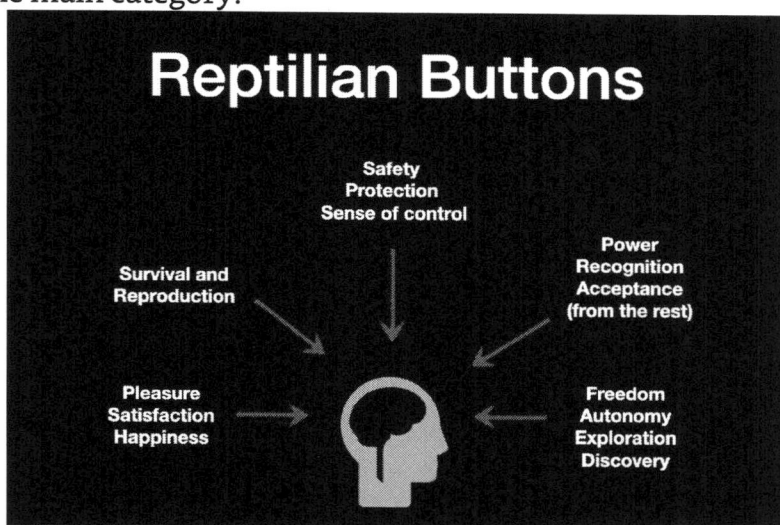

Reptilian Buttons

Safety
Protection
Sense of control

Power
Recognition
Acceptance
(from the rest)

Survival and
Reproduction

Pleasure
Satisfaction
Happiness

Freedom
Autonomy
Exploration
Discovery

These are the five reptilian buttons. You need to identify which one aligns best with your product or service, the one that you genuinely believe corresponds to what you're selling, and aim to engage the reptilian brain through it.

-        Survival and Reproduction: This is the most fundamental category, and in fact, the other categories derive their meaning from it. In reality, the majority of products and services can potentially fit into this category, even if it may not be immediately apparent. Let's take an example: you sell cars. Does it have anything to do with survival and reproduction? Absolutely yes. While it may also fit into other categories, let's focus on this one for now. Take Audi, for instance. They have quattro technology, an intelligent all-wheel drive system that may not initially seem relevant to the reptilian brain. But here's what matters: imagine you're driving and you encounter a sharp curve at high speed. Without proper traction, there's a risk of losing control and having a serious accident that could jeopardize your life and the lives of your family. However, with the quattro system, your car ensures exceptional grip even in the most challenging conditions. In that crucial moment, when the car is navigating that treacherous curve, the quattro system keeps it on track, preventing the accident. In other words, our quattro system can be the difference between life and death. Does the reptilian brain care? Absolutely.

Quattro all-wheel drive car.

Of course, there are other products, known as basic necessities, that primarily fit into this category, such as food and water. However, their importance is so obvious that the old brain easily understands it, whereas with other products it requires more effort.

- Safety/protection/ Sense of control. For example, a reliable alarm system or an insurance company perfectly fit into this category. They provide security, protection, and a sense of control, all aimed at enhancing survival and reproduction.
- Power/Recognition and Acceptance (from the rest of the pack). Training is an example that offers advantages over others, leading to power, recognition, and acceptance from the rest.

Training provides adaptive value within the "pack," which can be translated into power, recognition, and acceptance.

- Pleasure/Satisfaction/Happiness: Dining at a restaurant goes beyond mere survival and fits well into this category. When we visit a restaurant, especially an upscale one, we offer the old brain multiple benefits, particularly the pleasure, satisfaction, and happiness it provides.

- Freedom/Autonomy/Exploration/Discovery: While trips can also be associated with this category, they may have more prominence in the previous one (pleasure, etc.). However, the sale of a car has a significant component in this section. It can be a complementary way to guide the sale of a car.

As you can see, it is crucial to analyze your product or service and identify the primary benefit it offers within a specific category. Don't worry if your product or service fits into more than one category; it's not a problem. However, it is important not to mislead the reptilian brain, so you should focus on one category, at most two, and direct your efforts towards delivering a message that interests it. We will discuss how to construct that message later, but for now, remember that our equation includes benefits + characteristics of the reptilian brain (selfishness, need for contrast, tangible results, etc.). Our message is going to be very powerful, you'll see.

NEUROSCIENCE RESOURCES TO CAPTURE THE ATTENTION OF YOUR POTENTIAL CLIENTS

Capture the attention of your potential customers.

Throughout the book, I will emphasize the importance of capturing the attention of your potential clients. Remember, in every sales process, regardless of its nature, if you fail to capture your client's attention, you won't be able to initiate the sales process.

Therefore, your initial focus should be on capturing the attention of your potential clients. Once you have achieved that, you can then employ the strategies learned in this book to increase your sales success.

Attention is a primary and fundamental process. What exactly is attention? It can be described as the allocation of intellectual resources to a specific stimulus. If something captures your attention, you allocate those resources; otherwise, you simply don't. What fails to capture your brain's attention effectively doesn't exist. As Daniel Kahneman rightly argues, "we have a limited care budget (...) and if we try to exceed that budget, we fail" (Kahneman 2012). Tasks that require intellectual effort interfere with one another, so we are compelled to focus our intellect on one task at a time. Could you, for example, multiply 27 by 54 while reading and comprehending a paragraph from a book?

Attention can be conscious or unconscious, and in this book, we will discuss both as they are equally important. Our goal is to arouse the attention of any of the three brains, and if we manage to engage all three simultaneously, even better. Anything that fails to capture the attention of any of your three brains effectively doesn't exist. While it is possible to capture the attention of the reptilian brain without the other two being aware, if you capture the attention of the emotional or rational brain, you will inevitably capture the attention of the reptilian brain as well.

If you want to excel in sales, what do you need to know about customer service? First and foremost, capturing attention is akin to opening the door of a house. If you don't open it, you can't enter. Secondly, as human beings, clients can only focus their attention on one thing at a time. Thirdly, in this chapter, we will explore various attention grabbers. Lastly, we will utilize attention grabbers to highlight some of the benefits that the old brain finds intriguing, as discussed earlier. So, let's delve into some of the best attention grabbers that exist. Are you ready to learn about them? Let's get started!

ATTENTION GRABBERS:

1. Mini dramas: Create a mini drama that focuses on your client's concerns or problems. As David Ogilvy said, "If you sell fire extinguishers, start with the fire." It doesn't have to be animated or in video format; mini dramas can also be generated using photographs. Ideally, it should consist of two parts: a) portraying the world without your product (e.g., a house on fire in the case of fire extinguishers) and b) depicting the world with your product (e.g., a perfectly restored house with children playing after the fire scare). Using video format is more powerful as the brain is receptive to stories, and you can combine it with music to enhance its impact. A good example of a static mini drama is the Windex window cleaner or Mr. Cleaner.

2. Word games: The old brain is intrigued by word games. To utilize this attention grabber effectively, you need to be creative or consider hiring someone who is. The following ads provide examples of this attention grabber:

Here we have a case that illustrates the concept of a static mini drama very effectively. It succinctly portrays the world without the product and demonstrates how it resolves the issue.

3. Rhymes. It may seem absurd, ridiculous, and outdated, but neuroscience proves that messages that rhyme are better remembered. Moreover, this type of message is attributed with more intelligence and credibility (Tofighbakhsh 2000).

4. Stories. If you have the opportunity to interact with the client or record a short video, it is a great opportunity to tell a story. As mentioned before, the brain loves stories, and you should leverage this whenever possible. Building a story is not difficult, but it is crucial to consider the Peak-End effect. When evaluating events or stories, we tend to focus on two specific points: the peak of maximum emotional intensity (which can be positive or negative) and the outcome or conclusion of the story. Anything outside of these two points risks being completely ignored

(Kahneman D 1993).
Therefore, when constructing your story, ensure that the ending is happy, kind, and beneficial to the brain. Even if there are some negative aspects in your story (such as device noise or weight), make sure that the ending brings happiness. This way, the consumer's perception of the disadvantage will be significantly attenuated. This concept is supported by an interesting experiment conducted by Kahneman and colleagues, where volunteers were asked to immerse their hands in cold water. The duration and timing of the painful experience were varied, along with the ending (whether it ended with cold or a pleasant sensation of heat). Surprisingly, participants had poorer memories of short painful events that ended negatively compared to much longer painful experiences that ended positively. This experiment, along with others supporting this principle, demonstrates that humans, as well as other primates, evaluate events based on the end and the maximum emotional peak (Redelmeier DA 2003, Blanchard TC 2014).

Advice:

When constructing your story, it is crucial to ensure that the ending is happy, pleasant, and beneficial for the client.
Furthermore, as we will explore in the section dedicated to memory, it is intriguing to incorporate an improbable element that captures the brain's attention and leaves a lasting impression.

BIBLIOGRAPHY

Blanchard TC, WL, Vlaev I, Winston JS, Hayden BY. (2014). "Biases in preferences for sequences of outcomes in monkeys . . " Cognition **130** :289–299.

Kahneman, D. (2012). "Think fast, think slow." DISCUSSION .

Kahneman D, FB, Schreiber CA, Redelmeier DA. (1993). "When more pain is preferred to less. ." Psychol Sci. **4** : 401–405.

Redelmeier DA, KJ, Kahneman D. (2003). "Memories of colonoscopy: a randomized trial. ." Pain **104** : 187–194.

Tofighbakhsh, MSM a. J. (2000). "Birds of a Feather Flock Conjointly (?): Rhyme as Reason in Aphorisms." Psychological Science **11** (5): 424-428.

HEURISTIC SHORTCUTS OR SUBCONSCIOUS SHORTCUTS I

SUBCONSCIOUS SHORTCUTS

The brain constantly makes decisions to function and survive in the environment. The majority of these decisions are guided by internal rules that operate unconsciously. These rules, known as heuristic shortcuts, can be innate or learned throughout life. Heuristic shortcuts play a crucial role in the purchase decision because the old brain relies on them to draw conclusions. For instance, if the brain encounters an excessively lightweight metal watch, it may associate it with low quality based on the heuristic shortcut that something light is more likely to be flimsy. Understanding the existence and relevance of heuristic shortcuts in people's lives is essential for being a successful salesperson.

In simple terms, heuristic shortcuts are mechanisms that enable the brain to expedite complex decision-making processes. They are activated in situations where time is limited or when it's not beneficial to allocate additional mental resources (Tversky 1974). Our biases and preconceptions are closely linked to these shortcuts. Essentially, heuristic shortcuts estimate the probability of an event. For example, when the brain perceives something beautiful, it tends to assume it is good (Dion 1972). This generalization is often used without analyzing each individual case, and in most instances, the brain's assumption is correct.

While the use of heuristic shortcuts can lead to biased opinions, they are generally useful and effective in navigating complex scenarios that could otherwise leave us paralyzed. Our minds can be seen as intricate labyrinths, and heuristics allow the subconscious to navigate them, not always finding the exact exit but ultimately enabling our survival through evolution.

In the field of Neuromarketing, it is crucial to understand heuristic shortcuts because the majority of customers will rely on them when making purchasing decisions regarding your product or service. One of the most frequently utilized heuristic shortcuts in sales is the "Anchor Effect," which we will discuss in a dedicated section later on.

Under pressure, fear, or distress, the reliance on these shortcuts increases, bypassing the activation of the medial prefrontal cortex responsible for rational evaluation of the actual need for a product. Consequently, introducing elements of pressure such as limited-time offers or scarcity tactics can be effective. However, I personally do not support selling under pressure as it lacks honesty and falls into the realm of fear marketing, which I strongly discourage.

It's important to note that heuristic shortcuts belong to the subconscious (System 1 in Daniel Kahneman's theory), and when they are employed, the rational conscious part of the brain is unaware of the underlying reasons for the decisions made. Individuals may provide rational justifications for their decisions if asked, and in many cases, the explanations may seem plausible or even correct, but in other cases, they can be absurd.

Ultimately, these brain shortcuts form the basis of most of our purchasing decisions. They guide us in choosing between brands, emphasizing the significance of understanding and addressing them in the field of Neurosales. Companies invest significant efforts in creating new mental shortcuts, as exemplified by Coca-Cola's association with happiness, which we will delve into further in the book.

Coca-Cola has successfully created a heuristic shortcut (through associative learning) between its product and happiness, which has deeply permeated and become ingrained in the collective imagination. This association is so strong that functional magnetic resonance imaging shows activation in areas of the brain related to happiness. Interestingly, areas associated with memory are also activated, suggesting that this association has been learned through the company's advertising efforts.

Advice :

- *I highly recommend the systematic use of the anchor effect, which is one of the most fascinating heuristics for sales (see "The Brain and Prices" for more information).*
- *Can you create a heuristic shortcut for your business? The answer is an absolute yes, especially in today's technological era with our extensive communication networks. An excellent example of advertising aimed at creating a heuristic shortcut is the campaign for Blendec blenders (https://www.youtube.com/watch?v=lBUJcD6Ws6s). In this advertisement, you can witness one of these blenders disintegrating a phone, and they have consistently recorded videos showcasing the blender pulverizing various objects. The subconscious message that lingers is incredibly*

powerful: if that blender can pulverize an iPhone, just imagine what it can do to my fruit smoothies!

- *Therefore, if you want to establish a heuristic shortcut for your product or service, you must associate it with the desired quality or benefit you want to convey. For instance, if you sell insurance, you should link your brand with ultimate protection. If you specialize in selling chairs and wish to associate them with exceptional durability, create advertisements showcasing your chairs withstanding extreme weights and adversities while remaining intact.*

"PACK EFFECT"

I am deliberately going to start by explaining this effect to you because it helps me contextualize some of the essential aspects of the real scenario in which our brains developed and for which they developed.

The "Herd Effect" is also known as the Drag Effect, Fashion Effect, or Bandwagon Effect. And what does it consist of? Well, human beings are social animals, animals that, like other primates, have always lived within a peer group. Perhaps in the beginning, it was a herd, then a tribe, and eventually became a population. But the fact is that our brain has a strong dependence on that ancestral social structure. Herds have left an incredible imprint on us, and no matter how much we consider ourselves evolved and sophisticated beings, we are influenced - I dare say determined - by the mechanisms that the brain acquired to survive in a group.

We will talk about the herd in many places in the book because, without understanding what was happening there, we will never understand the irresistible subconscious desires of our brain. The point, regarding the herd effect here, is that we are innately programmed to follow the majority in virtually any area of conduct. We have an irrational tendency to accept as correct the ideas and reasoning of the majority, without prior rational analysis for such validation. We assume that the group, as a whole, knows something that we don't. Moreover, it has been shown that individuals who dissociate themselves from the majority and express points of view different from those of the rest of the group experience a pronounced activation of the amygdala, which translates into unpleasant emotions, fundamentally fear and insecurity. And it is this activation that we try to avoid at all costs, fleeing from autonomous initiatives and therefore following the herd.

Does it make sense? Without a doubt... The herd effect is still a very intelligent survival mechanism. If a group starts to run, they are most likely running for a reason, usually a danger. So it seems more sensible to follow them and get to safety than to be left alone in the face of danger.

The fact of following a trend, an ideology, also has a virtue with respect to our evolutionary program since the marginal individual runs the risk of being excluded, discriminated against, and therefore their chances of eating and reproducing decrease drastically.

Another curious effect also derived from life in a pack is that we perceive a lesser sense of threat when we know that many people are subjected to the same danger. And this is very useful within the pack because most of the potential dangers (e.g., any predator) are diluted among individuals. The more individuals there are, the more difficult it is for the tiger to eat you. Does the same thing happen when there is a housing bubble? And with major crises? And with bad investments in the stock market? Obviously not. Many of the dangers to which we are subjected today do not diminish because many individuals are threatened by it. But our brain irrationally continues to think so...

If you are a potential victim of a lion and you find yourself with only one mate, the chances of being eaten are 50%. But if you are with 20 mates, the chances drop to 5% and so on. However, many of the current dangers are not mitigated by the fact of sharing them with many individuals of the same species, although the brain continues to believe that they are.

Practical tips:

With the context we have outlined, in our digital world, there are numerous powerful tools with enormous influence that leverage the herd effect. The first and most obvious ones are social networks, which provide the perfect platform for leaders, or what we now call "influencers," to play their role and set trends for the herd to follow. The second set of tools is advertising campaigns, which also utilize this effect. Then there's a third category of tools that require special attention, and they are the spaces where both small businesses and large multinational companies need to invest their efforts: opinion platforms hosted on various applications (such as El Tenedor, TripAdvisor, etc.) and sales platforms (Amazon, eBay, etc.). More and more consumers, before making a purchase, rely on these platforms to learn about the evaluations made by other users. And this, dear reader, is where the herd effect comes into play...

Let's imagine we're making a purchase on Amazon, and we're hesitating between two alternatives for the same product. The first option has a rating of 1 star (out of 5) based on 14 purchase experiences, and the comments about that option are negative. On the other hand, we have a second alternative with a rating of 4.7 stars (out of 5) based on 453 purchase experiences, and it has highly positive comments. The prices are similar for both options. Which one do we buy? Obviously, the second option. We don't know the other users at all, nor do we know their needs or contexts, but we place significant trust in what the majority says. If the vast majority of people in the herd are favoring a certain food, let's say a fruit, it will have a much higher chance of being chosen over minority options. Similarly, if the majority of the herd rejects a fruit, it's unlikely for us to choose it.

Therefore, in our business, we must pay special attention to customer reviews. Undoubtedly, providing excellent service or having a great product is crucial, but it's not enough. We must encourage customers, especially satisfied ones, to share their opinions on the platforms that matter to us. For example, if you own a restaurant, when the meal is finished and it's customary to offer a liqueur or some kind of dessert (which, by the way, is a smart investment), it's a good time to ask for feedback and for customers to share their experience. This can be suggested elegantly with a note accompanying the liqueurs: "If you enjoyed your dining experience at our restaurant and think others could also enjoy an evening like the one you had, we would greatly appreciate it if you shared your experience on 'The Fork' application."

Outside of the digital world, there are also little tricks to leverage the herd effect. Once again, using an example from the hospitality industry, it's beneficial to have a sign in a restaurant that says, "Please wait to be seated." This sign not only helps manage tables and provides a sense of organization and customer service but also creates a small queue of customers, acting as a lure for others. Whenever we see a line at a place, we assume that some kind of reward is being offered in return.

In a similar vein, the tables that are usually filled first in a restaurant are the ones exposed to the public (visible to potential customers), while those in the interior are filled last. The goal is the same: to attract new customers by capitalizing on the herd effect.

SYMBOLIC VALUE

I t is undeniable that we attribute value to things that seem special to us. Products or services are worth more in our brains for what they mean than for what they really are. As you can anticipate, this is closely linked to the heuristic shortcuts mentioned above. Let's delve into it!

We will begin by illustrating the symbolic value of products with an experiment that will dispel any doubts you may have about it. What a group of North American neuroscientists did was give groups of volunteers a 10-euro wine and another 90-euro wine to taste, and then asked them which of the two wines they liked best. At the same time, they monitored the volunteers' brains using functional magnetic resonance imaging. The volunteers claimed that the wine they liked the most was the 90-euro wine, and they were not lying. When they tasted it, the medial orbitofrontal cortex in their brains was more strongly activated in the scans, which is related to pleasure, among other things.

The truth of the matter is that the researchers had deliberately switched the labels of the wines, so when the volunteers thought they were tasting the 90-euro wine, they were actually tasting the 10-euro one, and vice versa. What conclusion do we draw from this experiment? Well, a very simple one: the volunteers had assigned a symbolic value to the presumed 90-euro wine.

They had self-suggested and predisposed themselves to like it more. As a result, they enjoyed that experience more, and not only did they express it verbally, but the brain scans also showed that they genuinely enjoyed the experience more (Hilke Plassmann, 2008).

Therefore, while the quality of products and services is important, even more relevant is the symbolic value that we manage to convey through our product or service.

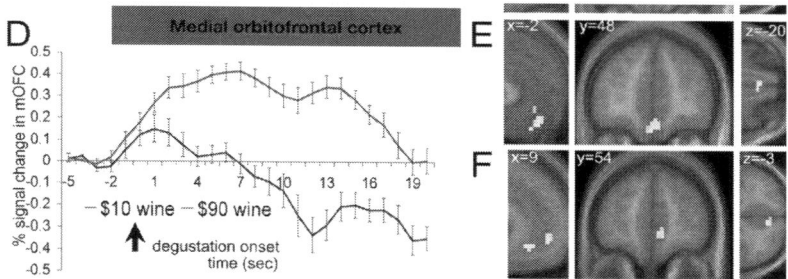

This experiment conclusively demonstrates that the brain is influenced by the symbolic value associated with a product. The consumer claims to enjoy the expensive wine more, and the functional magnetic resonance imaging also supports this, as it shows activation in the Medial Orbitofrontal Cortex. The beauty of the experiment lies in the fact that the researchers had switched the labels of the wines, so the expensive one was actually the cheap one, and vice versa.

Another good example of symbolic value can be seen in a Japanese fish called Seki saba. In the 1980s, this fish was considered a food for the less affluent, with a unit price of around 10 dollars. However, in 1998, the Japanese government decided to grant this fish a certificate of "superior quality food" and even distributed a guide to distinguish whether the fish was authentic or not. What happened to the value of the fish? Well, its price increased by 600%, and it is now considered one of Japan's delicacies. What has changed about the product? Absolutely nothing; the only thing that has changed is consumer perception, thanks to the symbolic value created around it.

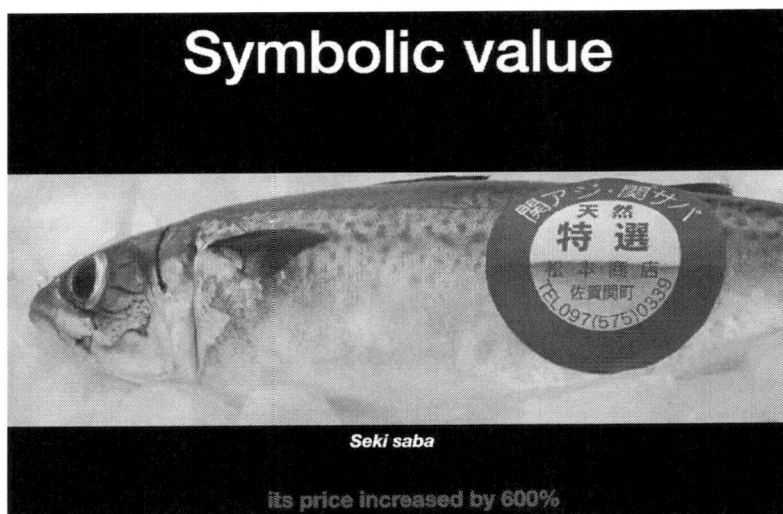

Symbolic value

Seki saba

its price increased by 600%

Seki saba is an excellent example that effectively illustrates the power of developing a strategy aimed at increasing the symbolic value of a product. The Japanese government implemented a remarkable campaign around a fish that was initially considered inexpensive, ultimately transforming it into a premium product with a value that skyrocketed by 600%.

The conclusion that we must draw from these two examples is that we should promote the symbolic value or perceived value of our product or service. Symbolic value is not something that needs to be explained to the consumer, but rather it is designed to entice them through the right strategy. If you analyze the leading brands in the market, you will immediately recognize those that have achieved a high symbolic value. When symbolic value is attained, the price of the product or service takes a backseat. Each product or service has its own symbolic value, and it is essential to identify and promote it. Essentially, as you can see, symbolic value is a heuristic shortcut that skillfully crafted by the seller to attract the consumer. Blendec mixers symbolize power and strength, while Coca-Cola represents happiness, and so on. Now, let's examine an example where the symbolic value has not been clearly understood, and that is in the design of the new water bottles for the Lanjarón brand. The symbolic value of bottled water is purity, and it cannot be packaged in a red bottle because the brain will never associate a red liquid (which is how water appears through the new containers) with this concept. I am convinced that they will have to discontinue the production of these bottles because it creates a dissonance in our brains when we see a red liquid being sold to us as pure water. The Solán de Cabras brand also uses colored bottles, but they choose a blue color that the brain can easily connect with pure water. In fact, the blue they use in their packaging conveys a message of purity and freshness. If Lanjarón's marketing department had understood the principles of Neuromarketing, specifically those related to symbolic value, and had analyzed the symbolic value they wanted their water to convey, they would have never chosen red as the color for their bottles. Once the brain attaches a symbolic label to a product or service, it becomes challenging to remove it. Essentially, by creating the label, the brain forms a heuristic shortcut. There is an experiment that clearly demonstrates the power of a recently learned symbolic value: a group of volunteers were shown two empty glass jars. They were instructed to fill them with sugar and then label one as "Sugar" and the other as "Cyanide." They were then offered a cup of coffee and told they could add sugar from either of the two jars. Interestingly, the majority of participants avoided the jar they had labeled as "Cyanide" (RUBIA 2000).

Advice:

You need to identify the symbolic value of your product or service. Once you have a clear understanding of it, you must create a mental shortcut in the consumer's mind (as seen in the case of Blendec mixers, capable of disintegrating a phone), and then develop an aura of exclusivity and authenticity around your product or service. In some cases, enhancing the symbolic value of certain products involves taking care of the packaging. A mediocre and careless packaging cannot align with a product with a high symbolic value. Therefore, it is an aspect that requires significant effort and attention.

You have to create symbolic value around your product. If you sell hamburgers, your hamburger must be special. When the consumer sees it, they should understand that they are not just dealing with anything. The quality of the products must be superior, but the presentation of the product is essential. Compare the presentation of the hamburger on the left and the one on the right. Even if the ingredients are the same, the symbolic value that the first one acquires makes the consumer perceive it as of higher quality than the second one.

If your product is not easy to wrap, you have to use your imagination. Let's take the example of a hamburger joint. You have a multitude of resources to generate symbolic value, such as advertising, decoration of the premises, music, aroma, etc., but we will focus on the hamburger itself. The symbolic value you can convey is diverse. McDonald's and Burger King have chosen the symbolic value of happiness, fun, and speed, but if I had an establishment of these characteristics, I would prioritize quality.

To create a symbolic value of quality, I would start with the place and various aspects beyond this chapter. Regarding the hamburger itself, I would take the following steps: First and foremost, I would be demanding with the ingredients, paying special attention to the meat and the bread. I would try to make the meat in my hamburgers exclusive in some way, and I would clearly communicate its origin.

The cook plays a fundamental role in the process, but what is truly critical is the advertising and, above all, the presentation of the product. A special hamburger cannot be served on a normal plate. The presentation must be consistent, using a plate or tray that evokes nature, such as a wooden or slate board. You can add extra details to enhance its premium character, like using a toothpick to hold the hamburger together, which could serve as a quality standard, reminding customers that they are not just eating any burger.

If you have the budget, it is recommended to have these elements designed by a Neuromarketing professional. However, if you don't have the resources, you can use the advice in this book to help you achieve it.

HALO EFFECT

B efore delving into the topic, let's explore a series of well-known and useful effects and heuristic shortcuts in Neuromarketing.

We'll begin with the 'Halo Effect,' which was first introduced by psychologist Edward Lee Thorndike in 1920 (Thorndike 1920). An illustrative example of this phenomenon is when we attribute positive characteristics to attractive people. In other words, our perception of a particular trait influences our perception of other traits about which we have no information. For instance, attractive individuals may appear smarter and kinder to us, even though we have no knowledge about their intelligence or kindness.

Numerous experiments have been conducted on this topic, but let's focus on one carried out in 1974 by Landy and Sigall (Landy 1974). In their study, neuroscientists presented a group of volunteers with a poorly written text. Later, the volunteers were shown a photograph of the woman who had written the text and were asked to rate its quality on a scale from 1 to 9. When the woman's face was attractive, the average score was 5.2. On the other hand, if the face was unattractive, the average score dropped to 2.7, and if it was neutral, the mean score was 4.7.

This effect is often observed with celebrities, as they are usually individuals who have achieved success in some aspect of their lives, leading us to idealize them to a certain extent. Consequently, even without knowing them personally, we tend to attribute positive qualities to them without having substantial data to form a well-rounded opinion. That's why attractive celebrities are frequently utilized in advertising campaigns, as we have a strong tendency to associate positive qualities with the products or services they endorse. A notable example is George Clooney endorsing Nespresso coffee. In such cases, the brand image is significantly reinforced by the 'Halo Effect' generated by George Clooney.

Furthermore, the 'Halo Effect' is not limited to people but extends to objects as well. For instance, in 2005, Apple capitalized on this effect with its iPod. The product was considered groundbreaking and disruptive at the time, and Apple heavily focused its advertising efforts on it. The iPod generated a 'Halo Effect' for the brand, leading to increased sales of other products. In fact, Apple's turnover rose by 68%.

HALO
EFFECT

Apple's turnover rose by 68%.

Apple employed a highly effective strategy by leveraging the 'Halo Effect.' The company concentrated the majority of its resources on advertising the newly launched iPod, which was a groundbreaking innovation at the time. As a result, the iPod overshadowed the sales of other products that had received less advertising investment. Apple's overall turnover experienced a remarkable exponential increase of 68%, and this growth was not solely attributable to iPod sales but also to the boost received by other products in the company's catalog, benefiting from the media attention.

The object or person that triggers the Halo Effect activates the nucleus accumbens, making us more receptive to the presentation of other products. If we have a positive memory of a particular brand, we are more likely to view other products or services from the same company favorably, even though we may lack knowledge to judge each product or service independently.

There is also a reverse effect known as the 'Devil Effect,' where we attribute negative characteristics to individuals or objects that fail to make a good impression on us. For instance, it would be challenging for us to trust a surgeon with tattoos up to the neck and twelve nose piercings to operate on our brain tumor.

Nestlé, the owner of the Nespresso franchise, is a company that has employed excellent strategies. They have utilized various Neuromarketing resources to promote the renowned coffee capsules. Undoubtedly, one of their most successful moves has been hiring George Clooney, who has effectively conveyed his aura of quality and success to the brand through the halo effect.

Advice:

- *Any business, regardless of its size, can benefit from the Halo Effect of one of its flagship products. To achieve this, I recommend identifying a product that has a strong reputation, such as the signature hamburger (let's say, "Japanese Hamburger"), and focusing the majority, if not all, of the advertising efforts on that particular product. The Halo Effect generated by the hamburger will subsequently lead to increased sales of the other products. It is crucial, however, that the hamburger meets the standards of excellence discussed in the previous section on "symbolic value."*

- *Additionally, if the budget permits, it is ideal to associate the brand or product with a well-known individual who embodies the values the brand seeks to represent, thus creating an aspirational image*

BIBLIOGRAPHY

Dion, K., Berscheid E. and Walster E. (1972). "What is Beautiful is Good." <u>Personality and Social Psychology,</u> **24** (3):285-290.

Hilke Plassmann, JOD, Baba Shiv, and Antonio Rangel (2008). "Marketing actions can modulate neural representations of experienced pleasantness." <u>PNAS</u> **105** (3):1050–1054.

Landy, D., & Sigall, H. (1974). "Beauty is talent: Task evaluation as a function of the performer's physical attractiveness. ." <u>Journal of Personality and Social Psychology,</u> **29** (3):299-304.

BLONDE, FJ (2000). <u>THE BRAIN DECEIVES US</u> .

Thorndike, E.L. (1920). "A constant error in psychological ratings." <u>Journal of Applied Psychology</u> **4** (1):25-29.

Tversky, AK, D. (1974). "Judgment under uncertainty: Heuristics and biases." <u>Science</u> **185** : 1124–1131.

HEURISTIC SHORTCUTS OR SUBCONSCIOUS SHORTCUTS II

THE BRAIN AND PRICES

As you may recall, in order for the purchase decision to be favorable, the level of loss aversion must always be lower than the anticipated reward.

If there is one direct factor responsible for triggering the loss aversion system, it is the price of our product or service. It is not a coincidence that in many countries, the bill is referred to as "the painful one." Setting the right price is a scientific endeavor, as numerous variables come into play. In this regard, I believe that calculating the price of your product should involve the strategies of classical economic theory (which falls outside the domain of Neuromarketing). This can be done by considering factors such as the unit cost price plus profit percentage, or analyzing pricing based on market dynamics and competition. Since this is not my area of expertise, I suggest leaving it to the specialists. However, what I can provide are insights and tricks within my discipline that I will present to you. After you establish the price of your product or service using economic theory tools, I recommend reading this section and considering whether any adjustments are necessary.

What happens if I set a very high price? If your product belongs to the Veblen category, it is essential for its price to be "prohibitive." In this case, you are on the right track. Veblens are a unique type of niche product where the price itself generates aspiration and serves as a status symbol. If you are interested in developing a Veblen product, you will find relevant information in the corresponding section. However, if this is not the case, as is typically true, pricing strategies must adhere to a different logic.

For non-Veblen products, if the price exceeds what consumers perceive as fair or reasonable, there will be a complete rejection of the product, leaving a lasting mark of disapproval that may be difficult, if not impossible, to overcome. In other words, even if you lower the price after setting it too high, it is possible that your product will never recover from that initial perception. It is crucial to avoid excessively high and unfair prices, as opposed to higher prices in general, which may simply lean the purchase decision towards a "no." For example, if a can of Coca-Cola were to cost 17 euros in a supermarket tomorrow, it would be doomed to failure because consumers would perceive it as unfair—an unacceptable price. It would be challenging for us to view the Coca-Cola brand in the same way again. In Brian Knutson's laboratory, functional magnetic resonance imaging was used to analyze how the insula (part of the loss aversion system) activates in response to unfair negotiations. On such occasions, the integrative center of the purchasing process is not even activated, and the feasibility of the purchase is immediately rejected (Brian Knutson 2007).

On the other hand, the price cannot be too low either, as it devalues the product or service being offered. A very cheap price is often associated with a loss of perceived product value or service quality.

Therefore, the price must be reasonable and aligned with the perceived quality of the product or service.

Even if you choose to set a high price, there are various strategies you can employ to make that price somewhat inconspicuous. A clear example is coffee. An excellent quality coffee, such as Lavazza Qualitá Oro, does not cost more than 17 euros per kilo. Typically, the coffees we purchase are around 9 euros per kilo. Now, let's delve into a brilliant move by Neuromarketing. In the context we have just described, where the highest range costs 17 euros per kilo and a more than acceptable range costs 9 euros per kilo, would you be willing to pay 66 euros for a kilo of coffee?

Do you think you have to be crazy, right? Or you have to have money to spare... well, dear reader, many of us have done it, and we have done it with absolute ingenuity. Have you ever consumed Nespresso coffee? Because if you have, you have paid about 66 euros per kilo of coffee... How did they manage it? Well, it's quite simple. The first thing they did was drastically reduce the amount of coffee in each box: 10 capsules per box, with 5 grams per capsule. They sell you 50 grams of coffee, which amounts to 10 servings. Each serving costs you approximately 0.33 euros. What your brain does is compare this price with the cost of a cup of coffee outside, without stopping to consider the price per kilo... Let's also remember that Nespresso has excelled in its advertising. You immediately associate it with George Clooney, and the "Halo Effect" does the rest...

We have another example to illustrate how to conceal a high price, this time with Lindt chocolates. Instead of comparing their price to other brands, let's analyze how they market their 99% cocoa chocolate. Firstly, it should be noted that the quality offered by Lindt is superior, and its price is likely justified. The distinctive feature is their 99% chocolate compared to other varieties. While I'm not familiar with the cocoa industry, I assume that producing a high-quality 99% chocolate is not easy, which justifies the higher price. However, Lindt must have some skilled advisors because they have cleverly overcome the price obstacle.

A 100-gram bar of 90% Lindt chocolate costs €2.65, whereas a 100-gram bar of 99% Lindt chocolate would cost €6. Clearly, presenting it this way would make it difficult to sell. Therefore, they have decided to sell a 50-gram bar at a price of €2.99. Now, how have they addressed the issue of the 50-gram bar appearing less substantial compared to its 100-gram "sister"? Well, they have used the same packaging for both, so when you see them, they look identical. They have ingeniously distributed the 50 grams of chocolate in an ultra-thin sheet (half the thickness of the 90-gram bar), which is "protected" by a thick golden-colored plastic that curiously weighs 50 grams. This approach achieves a dual impact: firstly, the "golden chest" packaging creates an appearance of luxurious exclusivity, and secondly, when you hold both the 90% and 99% bars, unless you read the packaging, you are unable to discern that one contains half the amount of chocolate than the other. It's a highly intelligent strategy.

Considering that 99% chocolate is very pure and typically consumed in smaller quantities than 90% cocoa, there is also a justification for the thin layer.

Lastly, regardless of the price you choose (excluding Veblen products, where a high price is part of their appeal), I advise you to utilize the following techniques to minimize the negative impact of loss aversion on the brain. When displaying the price of your product or service, use as few digits as possible. For the brain, it makes a difference:

€1,559.99 than € 1,559

The second option appears less distressing to you. Furthermore, it is not the same either:

€1,559 than €1559

And to further expedite it, it's even better to remove the currency symbol, as it appears shorter to the brain, reducing the feeling of loss aversion. Therefore, the transformation becomes:

1559 instead of €1559

Observe the final difference:

The computer on the right appears cheaper to the brain than the one on the left.

When offering discounts, you also need to be very clever. Imagine you have a product, regardless of what it is, that is sold in a 100 ml container and costs 100 euros. Now, you want to offer a deal where you provide 150 ml for the same price of 100 euros, which is essentially a discount of nearly 35%. The advertisement for such a product could simply state "35% discount," but that advertising would have a much weaker impact compared to if you said: "50% more FREE." Though economically it's the same, from a brain perspective, the second option is much more impressive. Rarely does the rational part of the brain start calculating the profit margin. Therefore, aim to make your trading strategies have the greatest impact on the brain by utilizing tactics like these.

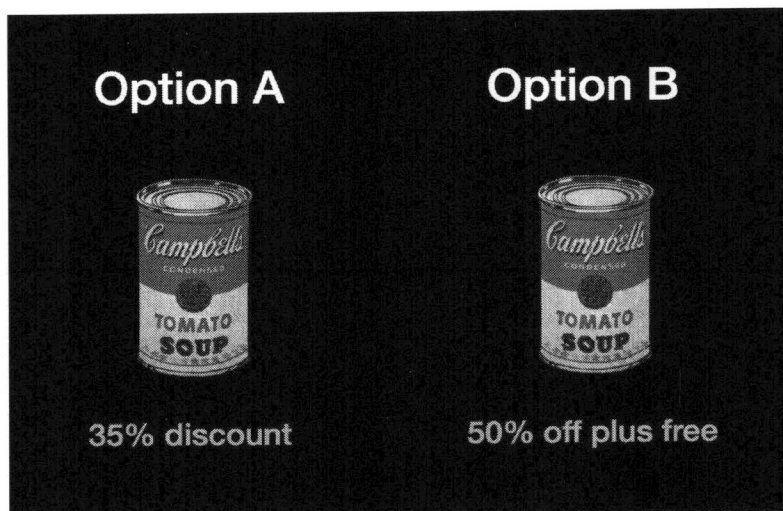

The offer on the right is much more appealing to the brain than the one on the left.

For some inexplicable reason, the number 9 has a magical effect on the brain. The rational part will never comprehend it, but empirical tests demonstrate that prices ending in 9 tend to result in higher sales. Therefore, when establishing a price, it is much more effective for it to end in 69 rather than 65.

Regarding the presentation of products, whether on shelves, in a promotional area within the sales room, or in a catalog, it is ideal to offer three purchasing options, each within its own price range. Two options are too few, while four or more can create confusion and make decision-making difficult. When we present three choices, we have an inherent tendency, as a general rule, to opt for the middle one. In other words, if we present options A, B, and C, the majority of consumers will choose option B. Generally, we are averse to extremes and feel more comfortable and secure when selecting the middle ground. At this stage, the most intriguing approach is to first present the most expensive option (taking advantage of the anchoring effect), even if it is significantly pricier. This strategy will greatly influence the selection of the product we intend to sell, which will be positioned in the middle.

You should always present three options. The brain naturally tends to favor the middle option. If we also utilize the "anchor effect" to promote this particular option, the likelihood of making a purchase will significantly increase.

"ANCHOR EFFECT OR ANCHORING EFFECT" (ANCHORIN G EFFECT)

What is the "Anchor Effect"? It is another mental shortcut (heuristic) through which the brain is heavily influenced by the initial numbers presented to it during decision-making. The original experiment was conducted by Nobel Prize winner Daniel Kahneman and his partner Amos Tversky (Tversky 1982). In this experiment, a group of volunteers was asked to estimate (with very little time) the result of the following calculation:

Group A: 8 x 7 x 6 x 5 x 4 x 3 x 2 x 1

A different group was asked the same question, but with the following calculation:

Group B: 1 x 2 x 3 x 4 x 5 x 6 x 7 x 8

In the first case, the average estimation was 2250, while in the second case, it was 510. The actual result in both cases is 40320, but it is interesting to note how the subconscious mind remains anchored to the initial numbers, which are the highest.

These two neuroscientists conducted another

experiment that confirmed the anchor effect. Volunteer subjects were asked to estimate the total population of African-Americans living in the USA, but just before this request, they were asked to randomly draw a number. If the number they drew was low, their estimation of the African-American population was also low, and vice versa. It is fascinating because they had not even heard a population estimate beforehand; the number they drew was entirely unrelated to the subsequent request made to them.

Practical tips:

· *In short: the brain tends to remain anchored to the values it encounters at the beginning. That's why in a catalog, products should be arranged in descending order of price. It is advisable to introduce an "anchor bait" to make the desired product appear less expensive.*

· *For example, if you have a restaurant and want to sell a T-bone steak for 22 euros, you should include an anchor effect with an "extra-super-special T-bone steak" priced at 30 euros, followed by your T-bone steak at 22 euros, and then another meat of lesser quality, for example, priced at 18 euros.*

AT THE EXTREME OF IRRATIONALITY: VEBLEN PRODUCTS

Normally, the price of a product is primarily determined by the supply/demand ratio. In this way, products with high supply and low demand tend to be cheaper, while products with low supply and high demand are typically more expensive. According to these principles, when the price of a product increases, its demand decreases because fewer people are willing to pay an excessively high price for it. However, there are exceptions to this rule, known as Veblen products. Examples of Veblen products include Bugatti cars and Rolex watches, which are clearly ostentatious in nature. Does purchasing such products align with rationality? Not necessarily. It is objectively unaffordable to pay 40,000 euros for a watch. However, these watches are sold based on an irrational psychological program that places value not on the utility of the watch itself, but rather on the social status associated with owning such a product—the "hierarchical position in the herd," so to speak. In this case, the Rolex watch serves as a symbol of power. These products are named after Thorstein B. Veblen, an American economist who was one of the first to explore the relationship between the consumption of certain goods and the pursuit of privileged social status.

Practical tip: How to create a Veblen product.

The Veblen products are a collection of highly exclusive products and services. While there is no foolproof formula for creating a Veblen product, most of them share common characteristics. The recipe for developing a Veblen product involves the following points:

1. *Your product or service must exhibit exquisite quality. There are few exceptions to this requirement. Exceptional quality is the foremost attribute that Veblen articles offer. While quality alone may not always justify the price, a future Veblen product must possess exceptional quality.*
2. *When it comes to branding, opt for a name that is easy to pronounce. While Veblen products are not exclusively associated with easily pronounceable brands, selecting such a name increases the likelihood of gaining entry into this exclusive club. Additionally, it is advantageous if the name carries a stamp of authenticity. In the Spanish-speaking world, surnames, particularly of Italian, French, and Spanish origin, are ideal. In the realm of fashion, consider brands like Christian Dior, Ferragamo, Versace, Prada, Fendi, Giorgio Armani, Ermenegildo Zegna, Louis Vuitton, Hermès, and Chanel. In the automotive industry, examples include Bugatti, Bentley, Ferrari, Lamborghini, Porsche, and so on. These principles apply to almost all sectors where*

Veblen products exist.

3. *Your product must acquire immense symbolic value. Design advertising strategies that elevate your product to a status far beyond its actual worth. A successful approach involves leveraging the halo effect of a renowned and influential celebrity, preferably one who exudes attractiveness. This association lends your product an aura of exclusivity.*
4. *The price of your product should be set high, further contributing to its symbolic value.*

* Firms with easily pronounceable names tend to be perceived as more credible. An experiment conducted involved two fictional Turkish companies issuing purported stock market reports. Deliberately, these reports contained conflicting information. Observers demonstrated significantly higher credibility towards the company with an easily pronounced name (Artan) compared to the other (Taahhut) (Anuj K. Shah, 2007).

Veblen Products

33.600 Euros

From a rational standpoint, it may not be justifiable to purchase a watch at such a high price. However, there exists a considerable number of individuals who desire these products. Clearly, these items serve as tools for establishing one's position within the social "herd" and are symbols of power.

SUBLIMINAL PUBLICITY

The concept of subliminal advertising originated in the summer of 1957 when James Vicary, an American market researcher, decided to incorporate the phrases "drink Coca-Cola" and "Eat popcorn" into frames of the film "Picnic." These messages were displayed for a duration of three thousandths of a second and repeated every five seconds. James claimed that the sales of Coca-Cola increased by 18.1% and popcorn sales by 57.8% in the cinema where the film was shown. He himself coined the term "subliminal advertising," but later he had to retract these results, confessing that he had fabricated the entire story, possibly due to the media pressure he faced. Subliminal advertising has raised significant ethical concerns in the field of neuromarketing as society has come to believe, despite Vicary's disavowal of the results, that the use of imperceptible instructions can condition human behavior. However, what is the truth behind subliminal advertising?

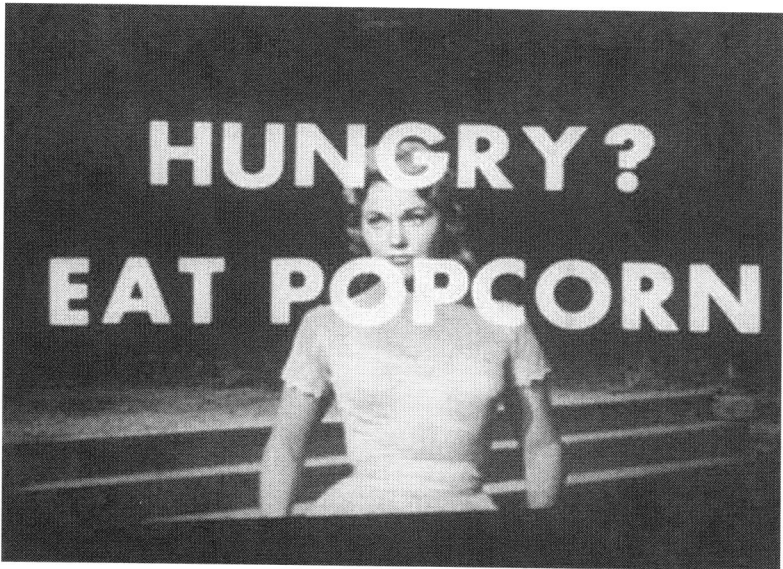

Original still from the movie "Picnic" which marked the controversial beginning of the world of subliminal advertising by James Vicary.

To begin with, let's define "subliminal." Stimuli (of any nature, visual, auditory, etc.) that are not consciously perceptible are referred to as subliminal. As a neuroscientist, I would categorize subliminal advertising into two divisions: stimuli that do not reach consciousness because they cannot be perceived (for example, word exposures lasting 3 milliseconds that the conscious mind cannot read), and stimuli that could reach consciousness but are not attended to due to inhibitory modulation, a phenomenon in neuroscience. For instance, imagine you are at a cocktail party engaged in a conversation and not consciously listening to the conversation nearby. Suddenly, someone mentions your name in that conversation. Your subconscious was processing the conversation, but inhibitory modulation caused you to ignore it and focus on the conversation in front of you. However, this inhibition is interrupted by an attention-grabbing stimulus—your name—causing the side conversation to enter your consciousness.

At this point, do subliminal messages influence customer buying behaviors? The answer, at least regarding messages that do not reach the conscious mind due to inattention, is emphatically yes. In the field of audiobranding, research has shown how environmental cues conditioned the purchase of wines (see audiobranding; North, 1999; North, 1997). Some buyers were aware of this influence, but the majority were not.

What about stimuli that do not reach consciousness because they are imperceptible? In 2006, a group of researchers from the University of Maastricht decided to replicate James Vicary's 1957 experiment. They chose Lipton Ice as the product and observed that subliminal advertising did work, but only with individuals who were thirsty (Karremans et al., 2006). Despite this, the results of the experiment were incredible.

Subsequently, other research teams exposed voluntary video game players to batteries of subliminal messages. One group was exposed to positive words such as "wise," "cunning," and "talented," while the other group was exposed to negative words like "senile," "depressing," and "sick." The players in the first group finished the game earlier than those in the second group (Glassman, 1999).

The conclusion we can draw is that subliminal advertising works, and it works remarkably well. Personally, I find the use of these hidden messages in advertisements not only illegal but also despicable. I firmly oppose the use of such techniques.

There is another type of advertising that treads the line between the conscious and the subconscious, known as product placement. These are products that appear on the big screen not as explicit advertisements but as part of the overall presentation. We can all recall instances of this type of advertising, such as a character wearing a particular watch or driving a specific car. Viewers are usually not attentive to these details consciously, but they register subliminally. It is not undetectable advertising, but typically viewers are engrossed in the plot of the film and not consciously paying attention to it.

Advertising through product placement is highly effective, but it must fulfill at least one of the following three requirements:
a) The product must be a coherent object in the development of the narrative plot.

b) The product must play an important role within the film's plot. A prime example is the Reese's Pieces candies in the movie "ET," which the child uses to entice ET to follow him. Another illustrative case is FedEx in the movie "Cast Away." c) The product should appear after a peak of positive emotions. This elicits positive feelings when the brand or product is seen again.

A good example of product placement advertising is seen in the movie "Cast Away" with FedEx. This placement is seamlessly integrated into the storyline and the emotional arc of the film.

There have been numerous experiments conducted on product placement advertising, but one in particular stands out due to its simplicity and effectiveness. In this experiment, adolescents are asked to surf the Internet, and as they navigate, pop-up windows appear. Some of these windows are accompanied by a discreet voice-over mentioning a brand. Interestingly, the teens did not pay much attention to these ads and did not remember them afterwards. However, the surprise came a week later when it was observed that their purchase intentions towards these products had actually increased, particularly when the advertisement had been accompanied by a voice-over (DIDIER COURBET 2015).

BIBLIOGRAPHY

Adrian C. North, DJHJM (1997). "In-store music affects product choice." Nature **volume 390** : page 132
.

Brian Knutson, SR, G. Elliott Wimmer, Drazen Prelec, and George Loewenstein (2007). "Neural predictors of purchases." Neuron .

DIDIER COURBET, M.-PF-CYJI (2015). "The footprint of advertising in the unconscious
." Research and Science : 50-56.

Glassman, NS, & Andersen, SM (1999). "Activating transference without consciousness: Using significant-other representations to go beyond what is subliminally given. ." Journal of Personality and Social Psychology **77** (6):1146-1162.

Johan C. Karremans a, Wolfgang Stroebe b, Jasper Claus (2006). "Beyond Vicary's fantasies: The impact of subliminal priming and brand choice" Journal of Experimental Social Psychology **42** 792–798.

North, AC, Hargreaves, DJ, & McKendrick, J. (1999). "The influence of in-store music on wine selections. ." Journal of Applied Psychology **84** (2):271-276.

Tversky, AK, D. (1982). "Evident impact of base rates." New York: Cambridge University Press .

NEUROPHYSIOLOGICAL ASPECTS OF MARKETING AND NEUROSALES

Mirror Neurons and the Limbic System. Emotions and empathy, crucial to sell.

BRANDING; TARGET: LIMBIC SYSTEM

"People will forget what you said, people will forget what you did, but people will never forget how you made them feel." - Maya Angelou

A s we have observed, the primitive brain makes decisions that are heavily influenced by the emotional brain (limbic system). Therefore, establishing an emotional connection with the consumer is crucial to establishing an effective bond.

In general terms, the process of building a brand is referred to as branding, and specifically, the field of Neuromarketing that aims to emotionally connect a brand with consumers is known as emotional branding. Although it is not an easy task, it is certainly achievable.

The first step is to determine the emotional personality of the client, and in this regard, it's important to acknowledge that each client is unique, highlighting the significance of segmentation and neurosegmentation. Within the marketing world, a longstanding debate has revolved around whether a brand should align with a client's real personality or with the personality the client aspires to have. What is your opinion? Neuroscience, once again, provides the answer. Studies indicate that it is more effective to align the brand with the consumer's real personality rather than their aspirations (Lucia Malar, 2011). When this alignment occurs, the consumer develops a stronger attachment to the brand. A prime example is the Dove brand. At a certain point, Dove made a conscious decision to embrace the real world, real women, rather than the idealized world of perfect women. By giving real women the prominence they rightfully deserved, Dove elicited an undeniable emotional attachment from many women. What Dove achieved went beyond women simply appreciating their soaps; it provided them with a psychological release. Through that iconic campaign, the brand's value skyrocketed from 200 million to 4 billion dollars (Berger, 2015).

The Dove ad campaign represented a significant turning point for the company. Women instantly identified with the message of embracing reality that the brand conveyed, leading to a strong sense of loyalty as a result.

Nowadays, whatever your business, you cannot

leave emotional *branding aside* . You have to build a brand with personality and try to get closer to the personality of your *target* , your target audience.

A clear example of well-worked emotional *branding* is that of Coca-Cola. The repeated, well-directed advertising of the brand has achieved something incredible : the mere sight of the can activates the dorsolateral prefrontal cortex, related to positive feelings, and concomitantly activates the hippocampus (Lucia Malar, 2011). , which means that this positive feeling emanates from our memories. Coca-Cola has managed to get us to see the can and associate it with positive things, there is nothing... and that is the success of Coca-Cola, and this is demonstrated by the innumerable experiments carried out where consumers are given to try Coke versus Pepsi. When these two products are tested blindly, that is to say: the consumer does not know what he is testing, what happens is that the less they tie. Of course, if the consumer sees the can of Coca-Cola... there is nothing to do, even if there is Pepsi inside! (Samuel M. McClure and Montague 2004) . Coca-cola advertising has made them not sell a drink, what they sell you is one of the most precious benefits for human beings: happiness.

We may never be able to reach Coca-Cola's level, but we have to make our brands arouse positive emotions.

What emotion does Starbucks arouse ? Does Starbucks sell coffee ? Not really , he sells you a mini vacation in a quiet place... What does telecommunications sell? Being able to connect with loved ones who are far from you... and so on with everything.

Practical tips :

Branding for your brand: How to increase emotional attachment with the consumer.

1. *What benefits will your product or service bring to the primal brain? (As we have seen in the beginning of the book.)"*

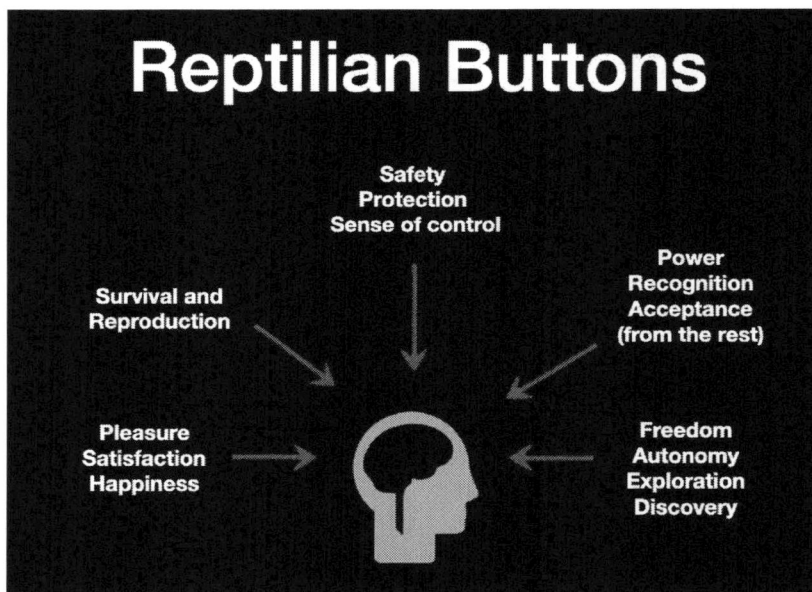

As we have seen previously, identify the main reptilian button of your product or service.

1. Once this benefit is identified, start creating an association between your brand and that advantage. Build symbolic value around your brand by evoking emotions.
2. Always consider your client as an individual rather than just a consumer. To achieve this, it is ideal to create an empathy map with your potential customers.
3. Make use of a compelling story (refer to

the corresponding section). Craft your own storytelling.

4. Create an authentic brand. People dislike inauthenticity or things that seem unattainable. Your brand's ideals should not be so lofty that potential customers feel excluded (Lucia Malär and Nyffenegger, 2011).

MIRROR NEURONS

Surely you have heard of them, but do you really know what mirror neurons are? Let's start from the beginning because it is extremely interesting. In 1996, something incredible happened in Parma. Giacomo Rizzolati and his research team studied a region of the brain in macaque monkeys that was responsible for motor functions, specifically the F5 region. This region was activated when the monkeys picked up an object. Additionally, they observed that when this region was damaged, the monkeys were unable to perform gestures of this type. In other words, they had identified the region of the brain responsible for certain types of movements, particularly those related to object manipulation.

While this discovery was important, it wasn't extraordinary enough to be a topic of conversation among friends over beers. However, they were greatly surprised when they stumbled upon another finding by chance. They discovered that the same region of the brain was also activated when the monkeys observed other individuals performing the same types of movements. What did this mean? It meant that watching someone perform an action triggers the same brain circuits as if we were performing that action ourselves. This discovery, along with numerous experiments conducted over the past three decades, led to the recognition of mirror neurons.

I want to emphasize this point because it is not trivial: when we see someone perform an action or experience a sensation, the same parts of our brain are activated as if we were experiencing that action or sensation ourselves. Subsequent experiments conducted in the laboratories of Giacomo Rizzolati, Tina Singer, and others were remarkable. They demonstrated that when we witness someone feeling upset or experiencing physical pain, we empathize, and the exact same neurons are activated in our brains as if we were the ones going through those emotions (Bruno Wicker, 2003; Engert V, 2014).

The good news is that this phenomenon also extends to positive emotions, and that's where the margin of maneuver for Neuromarketing comes into play. So, the next time you find yourself smiling when you see someone else smile, or feeling overwhelmed by another person's suffering, remember mirror neurons.

Research in this regard has gone much further, and functional magnetic resonance imaging has confirmed that not only observing the actions or feelings of others activates our mirror neurons, but even when we read about a sensation or an action, these brain regions are also activated within us. Are you aware of what I just said? Mirror neurons are not only activated by observing actions but also by viewing photographs or even reading. For instance, when a woman sees a model in a fashion magazine, her mirror neurons are activated, allowing her to imagine herself in the showcased clothes and adopting the attitude displayed by the model. This emphasizes the importance of paying attention to even the smallest details, such as a model's attitude, as these nuances can make a difference in how consumers perceive the purchase option.

Considering everything mentioned, we can and should use advertising to evoke pleasant sensations in potential consumers, which we want them to associate with our brand. Video is an effective medium for this purpose, but we can also employ images and, ultimately, phrases.

Mirror neurons have also been linked to imitation behaviors. An example is the classic Meltzoff reflex, in which a newborn sticks out its tongue and elicits a reciprocal response. This suggests that we have an innate tendency to imitate what others do, which may partially contribute to imitating the purchases of others. However, this phenomenon involves complex concepts, such as the well-known herd effect, among other factors.

Mirror neurons, along with loss aversion, are two crucial elements used in the examples I am about to share with you. The first example is a real case conducted by Patrick Renvoise and Christophe Morin, the authors of the book "Neuromarketing: Understanding the Buy Buttons in Your Customer's Brain" (Morin, 2008). They encountered a beggar holding a sign that read: "Homeless. Please help me" at the entrance of a restaurant in San Francisco. They gave him two dollars on the condition that he would let them change the message on his cardboard sign for at least two hours. If he was still there when they left, they would give him $5. To their surprise, not only was he still there, but he also refused the $5 and insisted on giving them $10. He had made $60 in the hour they were eating, whereas he normally made between $2 and $10. So, what did they put on the cardboard sign? They wrote the following: "And if you went hungry?" The power of that message was significant compared to the previous one because it directly appealed

to the viewer's emotions.

There is also an urban legend in the world of Neuromarketing involving a blind man who had a sign that said, "I am blind. I need to eat." They changed the message to "It's a beautiful day, but I can't see it." As you can see, in both cases, the difference lies in replacing a neutral text with an emotional message that, thanks to mirror neurons among other factors, compels the viewer to empathize with the person holding the sign. The fear of loss also plays a role (as we are all afraid of going blind or starving), and that helps drive the desired response (helping).

Therefore, it is essential to leverage this type of strategy in your advertising to engage the consumer emotionally and elicit the desired response.

THE IMPORTANCE OF A SMILE IN THE SALES PROCESS

T he smile plays a crucial role in human interactions as it creates a heuristic shortcut in the brain. Smiling produces positive reactions, primarily mediated by mirror neurons that have been observed previously, and increases attractiveness. Research conducted by the group of neuroscientist Roberto Cabeza from Duke University, using functional magnetic resonance imaging, has shown that seeing a smile activates the reward center of the brain. In their study, they discovered that when volunteers observed the faces of people smiling, the reward regions of their brains were activated. Additionally, the volunteers remembered the names of the people who smiled much better than those who did not (Cabeza, 2008).

Further research by Magnus Söderlund and Sara Rosengren (Rosengren, 2003) also discusses the concept of joy appeal, which refers to the attraction produced by a smile and how a salesperson's smile can evoke joy in the customer.

If you want to sell more, start with a smile.

Advice:

-       *One of the best tools you should use to increase your sales is to smile, both yourself and your workers. Smile naturally.*

BIBLIOGRAPHY _

Berger, M. (2015). "The power of brands." Research and Science : 45-49.

Bruno Wicker, CK, Jane Plailly, Jean-Pierre Royet, Vittorio Gallese, and Giacomo Rizzolatti (2003). "Both of Us Disgusted in My Insula: The Common Neural Basis of Seeing and Feeling Disgust
." Neuron **40** : 655–664.

Head, TT a. R. (2008). "Orbitofrontal and hippocampal contributions to memory for face-name associations: The rewarding power of a smile
." Neuropsychology. **46** (9):2310.

Engert V, PF, Miller R, Kirschbaum C, Singer T (2014
). "Cortisol increase in empathic stress is modulated by emotional closeness and observation modality." Psychoneuroendocrinology **45** : 192-201.

Lucia Malär, HK, Wayne D. Hoyer, & Bettina Nyffenegger (2011). "Emotional Brand Attachment and
Brand Personality: The Relative
Importance of the Actual and
the Ideal Self." Journal of Marketing
 Vol. 75 (35–52): 35–52.

Rosengren, MS da S. (2003). "The Smiling Face in Marketing Appeals and its Effects on the Cust." SSE/EFI Working Paper Series in Business Administration **2003:7** .

Samuel M. McClure, JL, Damon Tomlin, Kim S. Cypert, Latane´ M. Montague, and a. P. R. Montague (2004). "Neural Correlates of Behavioral Preference for Culturally Familiar Drinks." Neuron **44** : 379–387.

NEUROSCIENCE IN IN-PERSON SALES

I n-person sales deserve a special section. When you have the opportunity to meet with a client face-to-face, there are many aspects to consider in order to captivate the reptilian brain. Let's break them down one by one.

THE FIRST IMPRESSION

You know what they say, you only have one opportunity to make a good first impression, so you have to make the most of it. To begin with, you have to take great care of your image. Within this section, a fundamental aspect is the clothes you wear as it is the first thing the client's subconscious will evaluate. Remember the halo effect and never underestimate its impact. With all due respect to beggars, imagine walking into a car dealership and being served by a person who looks like a beggar. What would you think? Let's consider an even more sensitive context... Would you allow your 6-year-old daughter to undergo open-heart surgery performed by someone with 15 piercings in their ears, 3 earrings in their nose, dreadlocks down to their knees, and covered in lice with 4 skull tattoos? Let's not be hypocrites, the answer is clear... no. Do any of these characteristics determine their skill with the scalpel and knowledge of the human body? No, but once again, the halo effect rules in the subconscious. Therefore, it is essential that your image is the best possible. Of course, you have to follow the principle of empathy. For example, if you sell spray cans for graffiti artists, you cannot go dressed in a suit because you would sell much less than if you dressed like them. The same applies to other situations. When in doubt, it is always better to err on the side of being overdressed. Therefore, my advice is to carefully study how most of your potential clients dress and aim to dress slightly better than them. The halo effect has a relentless power. Unconsciously, another heuristic shortcut, we assume that a person who dresses very well (for example, in a suit) will possess superior qualities compared to one who does not.

Next, you have to pay great attention to your hairstyle as it is immediately associated with hygiene, and once again, we must consider the halo effect. Would we attribute good or bad qualities to a person with greasy hair and dandruff? Well, that's the point. Therefore, ensure that your hair is well taken care of. For women who dye their hair, it is important to regularly cover up visible roots as pronounced roots send a negative message to the subconscious, such as neglect or lack of cleanliness. If you are a man with thinning hair, it is best to keep it as short as possible as it creates a greater sensation of cleanliness and order compared to sparse and long strands, which convey undesirable sensations.

Now, let's address a sensitive but crucial topic: breath. It takes a lot of trust for someone to tell us that our breath smells. However, just because no one has mentioned it doesn't mean we are not affected by it. We are highly sensitive to odors, and I'm sure you have experienced the discomfort of encountering someone with bad breath. If you are a salesperson with halitosis, you are at a disadvantage. Therefore, I recommend seeking professional help from a digestive specialist and dentist. In the worst case, maintain excellent oral hygiene by brushing your teeth three times a day, using dental floss, and cleaning your tongue and gums as food particles can accumulate in the taste buds' crevices, leading to bacterial fermentation and an unpleasant odor. It is also advisable to use mouthwash or menthol spray. However, be cautious with chewing gum as it can be perceived as rude in certain contexts and project an image of arrogance.

Continuing with the importance of dental hygiene and appearance before discussing the smile again, let's emphasize the significance of teeth. Healthy, white, and clean teeth convey a sense of good health, hygiene, and order. If the person trying to sell us something has severely misaligned

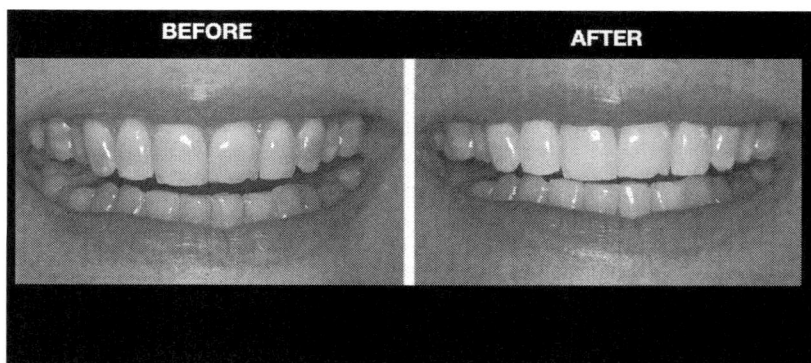

The brain utilizes teeth to generate heuristic shortcuts. Neglected teeth create a detrimental devil effect, and conversely, well-maintained teeth have a positive impact. The good news is that they can be fixed in almost all cases and will be one of the best investments we can make in ourselves. These examples demonstrate real cases, showcasing simple teeth whitening (top) as well as more sophisticated solutions for addressing complex dental issues (bottom two).

Advice:

If you have black or stained teeth, don't worry, there are excellent teeth whitening treatments available. It's best to visit a dental clinic that specializes in teeth whitening, and you'll be amazed by the results they can achieve. The most effective treatments involve hydrogen peroxide gels combined with LED light, which, when used with night splints, produce incredible results. It's possible that your teeth may become slightly more sensitive during the process, but it's manageable. Nowadays, the gels and toothpastes used in these treatments include ingredients that significantly reduce sensitivity, so it shouldn't be a problem.

Another aspect to consider is the use of glasses. If possible, try to avoid wearing them when selling. If it's unavoidable, opt for glasses with minimal reflection. Seeing the eyes is crucial for us as human beings. The expressiveness of the eyes conveys a lot, and in fact, credibility can be compromised if we cannot see our interlocutor's eyes clearly. It's not a coincidence that when we want someone to tell us the truth, we insist that they look us in the eye. Now, imagine the polar opposite—what would you think of someone trying to sell you sunglasses? Some companies have even chosen to co-finance corneal operations for their employees to eliminate the need for glasses, and they have found that it increases sales (Klaric 2017).

Another significant factor to consider is the perfume you wear. Major brands understand this well, and many of them (including a powerful car brand, whose name I will keep anonymous) require their salespeople to wear perfume. However, caution is necessary as overly strong perfumes can have the opposite effect. It's important to choose a perfume that is not too intense, and in any case, avoid using an excessive amount. You may already be aware of this, but the most effective technique is to create a "cloud" by spraying a small amount of perfume in the air and then walking through it. Alternatively, you can apply a small amount of perfume on the neck, décolleté (for women), the nape of the neck, and the inside of the wrists. This way, when you move your arms, the scent will be subtly dispersed in the surroundings. Selecting the right perfume is an art, and although I won't delve into it in this book, it holds tremendous importance.

And remember, never forget to smile at any time! (refer to the previous section)

CUSTOMER INTERACTION

The principle of empathy is highly effective when engaging with clients. It involves adapting and, to the extent possible, imitating their mannerisms, verbal and non-verbal language, and even their style of dress. This approach helps establish a deeper connection with the client. When we perceive someone as similar to us, we tend to relax, let our guard down, and become less suspicious. This, in turn, leads to better sales outcomes.

An essential skill, which only a few salespeople master, is the ability to listen. Remember this crucial point: by actively listening and asking insightful questions, you can uncover the genuine needs, concerns, and problems of your customers. In our book, we dedicate a special section to the ethics of neuromarketing, and I can tell you that the greatest honesty in sales lies in listening. It's not about selling anything and everything, but rather ensuring that a good salesperson sells what the customer truly needs. This approach leads to triumph, especially in the medium and long term.

For instance, if you are a car salesman, your first step is to listen and ask a series of questions to form a mental picture of the customer's requirements. What does the customer's brain, the one seeking to purchase a car, want or need? Do they require additional space due to having a large family? Are they seeking fuel efficiency for frequent travel? Do they desire a new status within their social circle through their car choice? Once the true needs have been identified, that's when you can apply the tools you've learned from this book to effectively appeal to the primal brain and tip the balance towards making a purchase.

In any sales process, the ability to listen is essential. You need to identify your client's fears and help them overcome those fears through your product or service. Unfortunately, the majority of merchants do not take the time to listen. Don't be one of them.

Deep down, in the majority of cases, what we need to identify are the fears of the customer's brain. Are they afraid that their belongings won't fit in the trunk? Are they concerned about the car's fuel consumption? Do they worry that the car won't position them where they want to be in their social circle? Identify their fears and offer a suitable solution.

During the sales process, the sense of touch is also important. How the salesperson touches or refrains from touching the customers can make a difference. This is a delicate area, beyond the scope of this book. However, it's important to navigate it carefully because while controlled and strategic contact can build trust, excessive or clumsy contact can have the opposite effect. For example, when shaking hands with a customer, it can be helpful to lightly touch their arm with the other hand. However, if the salesperson is a man and the customer is a woman, it is recommended to limit this contact to the palm of the hand with the arm (not the entire hand).

HOW TO CREATE
A FAVORABLE
ATMOSPHERE
IN SALES

I n in-person sales, there is an interesting tactic that can be used: offering pure chocolate (70% to 99% cocoa). Research suggests that consuming cocoa can improve mood and promote a more reasonable mindset. Therefore, as a practical tip, if you want to create a more cordial and friendly negotiation environment, consider offering cocoa. Approach it naturally and use a white lie, such as saying you received the chocolate as a gift. The intention is not to deceive but rather to relax the emotional climate of the negotiation.

Chocolate contains various compounds, including anandamide (an endogenous cannabinoid), phenylethylamine (a neuromodulator associated with certain physiological processes like falling in love), tryptophan (an amino acid involved in serotonin synthesis), caffeine (a stimulant alkaloid), and theobromine (another alkaloid with mild physiological effects). However, it is challenging to attribute the properties of cocoa solely to these molecules due to their small concentrations. The release of endorphins triggered by the intake of pleasant foods, like chocolate, likely contributes to the state of well-being (Benton D1, 1999).

Another interesting approach, if the opportunity arises, is to negotiate over breakfast, lunch, or dinner. Sharing a meal can create a special camaraderie that is difficult to achieve in other settings. It reflects our instinctual tendency to trust those with whom we share an intimate moment like a meal. Moreover, it is a relaxed and pleasurable moment where the brain's reward center is activated. This provides an ideal opportunity for potential clients to open up emotionally and express their needs, fears, and concerns with greater frankness. A skilled salesperson can use this occasion to conduct a comprehensive needs assessment and offer appropriate solutions.

However, it is important to note that alcohol significantly alters decision-making. Under its influence, individuals tend to be more daring and underestimate risks. Therefore, it is advisable to never engage in business negotiations while under the influence of alcohol.

YOU HAVE TO ACCEPT MISTAKES (AND LEARN FROM THEM!)

I f a client comes to you arguing that your product or service has not been good, and in reality it has not been, do not try to discredit the client; on the contrary, you must agree with them, first out of honesty and then out of intelligence (honesty sells a lot, never forget that). Of course, if you consider that your company has made a great effort to improve - and it has - the next thing is to make them see it and demonstrate it.

For example, imagine that you have a chain of florists and a customer arrives complaining because their order was late or arrived in poor condition. You have to quickly analyze the situation in the light of biology: this person has given flowers to someone because they want to express care, love, and desire to be with that person (to put it more directly, they are deploying their unconscious strategy to ensure that person chooses their genes for reproduction rather than someone else's). The fact that the flowers arrived late, in poor condition, or didn't arrive at all has seriously damaged their interests, and you don't even know if it has jeopardized their relationship (the flowers might have been intended to reconcile, and if they never arrived, the relationship may have worsened).

Therefore, the first thing you have to do is admit the mistake and apologize. It is the only way to calm down the angry and rightfully so reptilian brain. The next thing you have to do is reward them in some way. You could refund their money, but what would truly repair the damage caused would be to reward them with the benefit they were seeking: making an impact on their partner. Therefore, the smartest thing to do would be to send their partner a free flower arrangement, slightly more extravagant than the one they originally ordered, making it clear that their partner placed the order on time and correctly, but that it was a company error that caused the problem. A very elegant additional reward would be to say: "We have identified the error and we are working to ensure that something like this never happens again under any circumstances. As a gesture of our commitment, we offer you a floral decoration of equal value to the one you initially ordered."

In this way, the client achieves the benefit they were looking for and will regain trust in your company. Never think of the cost of this action as an expense, but rather as an investment. A dissatisfied customer will not only refrain from making future purchases, but they may also spread negative publicity about your company, resulting in the loss of potential customers.

A good example of this practice is seen with phones sold by the Google company. They offer a two-year warranty, which is a lengthy period for such dynamic technology. If the phone fails within those two years and they are unable to replace it, they refund the full amount of the phone's cost. I have witnessed this firsthand. It's a highly appealing message for consumers and a smart long-term strategy. It's nearly impossible to find dissatisfied customers.

THE COMMUNICATION PROCESS.

Two crucial aspects must be differentiated within this section: the message that is transmitted and how it is disseminated.

Regarding the message: I have dedicated a special section in the book on how to construct them, but here I would like to emphasize that selling has an important pedagogical component. Once you have identified the customer's needs and are ready to present the benefits of your product or service, patience is key. The client, in general, is much more intelligent than many salespeople assume, but they assume that you know more about your product or service than they do. Therefore, you must be patient, explain the benefits carefully, and never make the client feel inadequate or uninformed. You will be sharing information in one order, while the client's brain may process it in a different order, so you may need to repeat things several times. Do it with care and respect. The client must always feel important, and you must make them realize that their problem or fear is not exclusive to them, although you should avoid telling them that everyone has the same issue. Above all, show genuine interest in their problem as a good professional would.

When the information is complex and disruptive to the market, a good strategy is to provide the client with a concise dossier or brief technical file. This document should be attractive, simple, and pedagogical. Utilize the knowledge from this book in its design, and if possible, seek assistance from a graphic designer. Include the benefits of your product or service and give the client the opportunity to study it carefully at home. If you have favorable opinions from third parties, such as newspaper reviews or testimonials from other clients, it would be ideal to include them in this document. The credibility of your product or service will be significantly higher when supported by third-party endorsements rather than just your own claims. Therefore, one of your initial objectives should be to gather this type of evaluation to showcase to customers. Similarly, displaying third-party opinions in your place of sale or on your business website can be very useful. You don't need extravagant sophistication for this; sometimes a corkboard with newspaper clippings or printed sheets with customer reviews can make a strong impression. Remember, written information carries greater credibility. You can claim that the car you sell is the only one on the market with the X security system, but if you provide the client with that information in writing, it will have a significantly greater impact, as written information is seen as more trustworthy by our subconscious.

Regarding the transmission of the message: how you deliver the message is crucial. It's similar to telling jokes. A great joke can be ruined by a poor joke teller, while a mediocre joke can be hilarious when delivered by a talented individual. The same applies to the sales message. It is essential to know how to construct it and understand the neurosales tools to effectively reach the reptilian brain. However, you must also possess the necessary skills to transmit the message forcefully. According to Jurgen Klaric (Klaric 2017), in a communication process, body language accounts for 55% of your message, 28% is conveyed through intonation, and only 17% is the actual message itself. While non-verbal language and intonation are beyond the scope of this book, if your future depends on in-person sales, you should consider training yourself in these skills to become more effective.

HOW TO CONSTRUCT YOUR MESSAGE

I don't think that at this point in the book, when constructing the message, you fall into the (widespread) mistake of talking about your company, your firm, yourself... That doesn't matter to the client's reptilian brain. The message that you transmit to him must always focus, I insist, always, on the benefit that you are going to give him (see the corresponding section), never forget that the reptilian brain is terribly selfish.

With that perfectly clear, the first thing you have to do is choose a good attention grabber. Without it, it is difficult for the brain to stay and listen to the rest of the message (see the section corresponding to how to capture attention).

Once you have your attention grabber, remember that customer attention is very limited. Remember the saying: "If the good is brief, it is twice as good." A mistake is trying to fit too much information into your message. The message not only has to be brief but also has to be simple. This point is also crucial, and pay close attention to it because it is clearly counterintuitive. If you want your message to seem credible and intelligent, you must simplify as much as possible. When you try to use pretentious language, credibility is lost, and it also denotes a lack of intelligence (Oppenheimer 2006). Therefore, even if you are tempted to do otherwise, use as simple language as possible.

Well, you have already captured the customer's attention, you have built a short, simple message, and now you have to make it strong. To construct an effective message, it is very useful to insert a combination of the following words, as they are some of the most forceful terms for the old brain:

I, we, you, you + Imagine, build, entertain, transform, create, do, remember, enjoy, discover, win, feel, deserve, act, power, achieve, protect, dominate, conquer, reach, achieve, control.

Yes, exclusive, new, offer, original, only, unique, value, more, less, better, extra, solutions, instant, benefits, fast, easy, first, fresh, last, safe, limited, total, proven, professional, important, powerful, incredible, success, intelligent, save, famous, essential, complete, never, always today, now, guaranteed, urgent, opportunity, prize, attention.

Once you have all that, you have to introduce elements that allow your message to be remembered. As we see in the memory section, one of the best elements for something to be remembered is something implausible, something that really draws the brain's attention and therefore gets stored. The implausible can be used to take advantage of introducing symbolic value to your brand.

For example, a brand of shoe polish uses an ingenious imagery in which a shoe cleaned with its product becomes the rearview mirror of a car, implying that it is so clean and shiny that it can be used as a mirror. This implausible concept creates symbolic value.

PYRAMID OR HIERARCHY OF HUMAN NEEDS

At this point, you should have ingrained in your mind that the primary concern of the reptilian brain is survival and reproduction. Around these basic yet crucial motivations, other secondary and tertiary needs arise. Thus, a hierarchy of needs can be observed. This concept was introduced by American psychologist Abraham Maslow, who proposed the "Theory of Human Motivation" (Maslow, 1943). According to this theory, as individuals satisfy their basic needs, located at the base of the pyramid, they develop higher-level desires and needs situated at the top. The significance of this concept lies in the fact that individuals only concern themselves with higher needs once their lower needs have been fulfilled.

The pyramid consists of:
1. Basic needs: These encompass the most essential physiological requirements such as breathing, hydration, eating, sleeping, excreting, and being free from pain. In other words, within the context of our discussion in this book, these needs pertain to survival and immediate reproduction. Failing to

fulfill these immediate needs puts our short-term survival at risk, rendering it impossible to focus on anything else until these needs are met.

2. Safety and security needs: These needs are also considered fundamental and arise once the previous needs have been fulfilled. They encompass physical safety (health), protection (home), and access to resources (money). While they are still related to survival and reproduction, they are not as immediate and fall within the short-term category.
3. Social needs (affiliation): These needs are connected to our social life, such as having a partner, friends, and being socially accepted. They are linked, in the long term, to survival and reproduction. To understand this, think in archaic terms when humans lived in groups. An individual who is not socially accepted by the group faces the risk of exclusion, significantly reducing their chances of survival and reproduction. While these needs are important, they are not as immediate as the previous ones.
4. Esteem and recognition needs: This is where the hierarchical position within the group comes into play. As you know, the higher an individual's position in the group, the greater their chances of survival and reproduction. It provides better opportunities for mate selection and passing on their genes (as discussed in the previous chapter).
5. Need for self-actualization: This need involves

developing one's full potential as an individual. It can be seen as a deeper need compared to the others and is often challenging to achieve.

Advice:

If you encounter a person in the desert who hasn't had a drink for a day and a half and has a million dollars, what do you think would interest them more: a house or a quart bottle of water? Well, the same principle applies to everything else. Analyze the context of your potential customer as deeply as possible, place them within Maslow's pyramid, and evaluate whether any of the products or services you offer meet their needs at that particular moment. This concept is closely tied to market segmentation, and therefore, you should incorporate the hierarchy of needs as one of your filters.

BIBLIOGRAPHY _

Klaric, J. (2017). Sell to the mind, not to the people Paidós Empresa.

Maslow, AH (1943). "A Theory of Human Motivation." Originally Published in Psychological Review **50** : 370-396.

NEUROPHYSIOLOGICAL FOUNDATIONS OF MEMORY: MEMORY CONSOLIDATION, IMPRINTING YOUR PRODUCT IN THE CONSUMER'S MIND FOREVER.

NEUROPHYSIOLOGY OF CONSUMER LEARNING AND MEMORY

The knowledge we have gained through neuroscience studies has led us to conclude that one of the most valuable indicators for evaluating the effectiveness of an advertising campaign is the level of recall it generates in consumers regarding the promoted product or service. While recall is not the sole determining factor, as consumers may remember a brand without intending to make a purchase, it is certainly a crucial step in the process. So, what resources can we employ to optimize the memorization of our product or service in potential customers? Undoubtedly, we need a basic understanding of the neurophysiology of learning and memory.

From a practical standpoint, learning and memory can be considered as two interconnected stages of the same process. Learning refers to the acquisition of new information or skills, while memory pertains to the ability to retain and recall that acquired knowledge or skill. It is generally unproductive to learn something new without the ability to retain and utilize that learning in the future.

The significance of these processes in the realm of sales is undeniable. Let's consider a consumer standing in front of a supermarket shelf, faced with numerous product options. The brand's ability to leave a lasting memory imprint and associate it with positive sensations and emotions is pivotal in influencing the consumer's decision-making process. Hence, the memory that an advertised product leaves in the minds of consumers holds immense importance.

The majority of strategies outlined in this book are crafted with the intention of ensuring that, when consumers find themselves at the pivotal moment of choosing between your product and competitors', they opt for yours. To achieve this, it is essential that your product has made a lasting impression in their minds.

Both memory and learning encompass a vast theoretical framework that surpasses the scope and objectives of this book, so we will need to simplify their treatment significantly. Forgive me, those who are well-versed in the subject, but we must be pragmatic.

Let's recall the ultimate goal: for consumers to remember our product and associate it with positive sensations and emotions that motivate them to consume it.

Learning is a highly intricate process with various classifications according to theorists. We will focus on a specific type of learning widely used in Neuromarketing: associative learning. You may have studied Pavlov's classic experiments with his dog and the salivation response to the bell (although, in reality, Pavlov used a metronome). He conditioned hungry dogs by repeatedly pairing the sound of the metronome with the presentation of food until the dogs began salivating merely at the sound.

Associative learning should not be underestimated. Let's briefly discuss a cruel experiment conducted in 1920 known as the "Little Albert" experiment, carried out by John B. Watson and Rosalie Rayner at Johns Hopkins University. They selected a peaceful and healthy eleven-month-old boy who exhibited no fears towards any object or animal. However, the researchers introduced a loud noise (produced by hitting a hammer against a metal sheet) simultaneously with the presence of a white rat. After several repetitions, the child began crying inconsolably only in the presence of the rat, and eventually extended his fear to other animals and objects resembling the rat. It goes without saying that this experiment, with its negligible ethical background, would be unrealizable today. Nevertheless, it serves as strong evidence of the power of associative learning.

While the associations employed in Neuromarketing

today are much subtler, they are no less effective. An intriguing example is the association that the Red Bull brand has made between their product and the experience of adrenaline rushes and accomplishing seemingly impossible feats. The Red Bull Effect highlights many significant aspects of Neuromarketing. Initially, pre-marketing tests conducted in 1984 revealed that over 50% of the volunteers found the product unappealing. However, the Austrian billionaire Dietrich Mateschitz, the creator of Red Bull, disregarded market analysis and instead invested heavily in an advertising campaign with a well-defined strategy. Red Bull positioned itself as an energy drink that enables consumers to tap into enhanced power and extraordinary physical and mental states, allowing them to overcome challenges they couldn't tackle without the drink. The company developed numerous advertising campaigns associating the brand with incredible achievements, and today, Red Bull sponsors extreme athletes capable of awe-inspiring feats. Are we immune to such messages? Not at all. A strong association has been established between the drink and the possibility of performing extraordinary acts (as symbolized by the famous "Red Bull gives you wings" slogan), leading to a continuous increase in sales. The company has maintained a steadfast advertising policy, allocating 25% of their profits to this endeavor.

Coca-Cola has pursued a similar campaign to associate their drink with happiness, and it's safe to say that their efforts have been fruitful. They have succeeded in triggering positive feelings in us when we see a can of Coca-Cola, activating the dorsolateral prefrontal cortex associated with positive emotions (Lucia Malar, 2011). Another common tactic in soft drink advertising is linking a specific beverage to quenching thirst. The objective is clear: when consumers feel the need to quench their thirst, they instinctively desire that particular soft drink. As you can see, associative learning is a significant factor.

We mentioned earlier that learning and memory are two phases of the same process. How does memory function?

The brain is far from being a video camera that faithfully records reality as it unfolds before us. We must never forget that its primary function is survival and reproduction, and it excels at learning and remembering important information for these purposes. While it is often said that "knowledge has no physical space," recent research suggests otherwise, although this topic remains the subject of intense debate. Nevertheless, it is evident that our memory capacity is not limitless, and we must be selective about what we store. The ability to memorize must be accompanied by efficient access to information. Having a wealth of information stored would be futile if it took three minutes to retrieve it. In terms of survival, such a delay would be disastrous. Imagine encountering a tiger and your brain taking three minutes to process the information and reach the conclusion: "Tiger, a highly dangerous animal, it is advisable to remain still." It would be absurd, wouldn't it? An agile and efficient system is necessary. Besides, do we really need to store every piece of information that comes our way on a daily basis? If you engage in honest reflection, you will realize that the majority of information passing in front of us is irrelevant for survival, making it pointless to retain such information. For instance, consider being stopped at a traffic light while pedestrians walk by. Would it make sense for you to memorize the details of each person's clothing or the license plates of the cars in front? The brain memorizes what is crucial for monitoring the environment for potential dangers and opportunities that affect survival and reproduction. Over time, it develops a fairly accurate understanding of the environment under those circumstances. We learn throughout life by "collecting" patterns. When new patterns align with existing ones, they are ignored, but when new patterns emerge, they are stored. For example, a pattern could be that sparrows fly and are generally harmless—a pattern learned and remembered indefinitely. However, if the brain witnesses a sparrow pecking someone's eye, it encounters a new pattern, which it immediately acquires and incorporates into future interactions with such animals. Therefore, it can be said that the brain memorizes things that capture its attention. When faced with a situation, it compares it to past experiences. If the circumstances are very similar and offer no new insights, it is likely to be forgotten. However, if the situation is markedly different and intriguing, it captures the brain's interest, leading to better retention. Events with emotional significance also have a profound impact and are not easily forgotten. The higher the emotional intensity, the more challenging it is for the event to fade from memory (as exemplified by how we all remember where we were during events like 9/11—its emotional impact on any ordinary person was profound, and the brain stored it vividly).

We easily memorize things that capture our attention because they are novel (and we subsequently store them in our memory) or because they have a strong emotional impact.

Therefore, as a practical application, if you want your product or service to be permanently remembered by your potential clients, you need to incorporate elements that capture their attention. Moreover, if these elements are emotionally charged, it will be even more effective. I strongly recommend focusing on the emotional aspect.

So, how can we achieve this? The best approach is to connect emotionally through storytelling. Remember that the brain loves stories—it craves them, in fact. If you present the brain with fragmented pieces of information, it will naturally seek to make sense of them and create a story. It's better to provide the story directly so that it can be easily retained. A great example that encompasses all these characteristics is the advertisement for "Stratos" chocolates by the Norwegian factory, Nidar. You can easily find it on YouTube by searching for "Stratos ad."

This ad combines an implausible scenario that grabs the brain's attention—specifically, a child performing adult tasks—with a strong emotional component. Additionally, it is presented in the form of a story. Once you've watched this advertisement a couple of times, it becomes difficult to forget. What's even more interesting is that if you encounter the brand in a supermarket, surrounded by various chocolate bars to choose from, there will be a connection between your emotional brain and your reptilian brain, making the option of Stratos chocolate bars more likely to end up in your shopping cart.

Stories can be improbable, and I highly recommend making them so in order to enhance memorization (similar to the Stratos commercial). However, they must always be coherent. For example, if you are telling a story about Santa Claus in Lapland, it's acceptable for Santa's reindeer to fly (even though it's not plausible). However, the sequence of events in the story must be logical—Santa Claus leaves Lapland with gifts and delivers them to each child, and it could never be the other way around.

The more surprising elements you introduce into the story, the more easily the brain will grasp it. That's why in the world of advertising, stories are often told with interspersed surprising events to capture the brain's attention. If you're not already doing this, I strongly encourage you to start.

To intensify the emotional aspect, it is essential to use good music as it greatly enhances the emotional connection associated with the visual component. To understand the importance of music, try watching the Stratos ad without sound and observe how much impact it loses.

Example of something implausible that will be perfectly memorized by the brain. As you can see, you need to tap into your imagination, but the outcome is worth it. (Image created by MrSkullking).

BIBLIOGRAPHY

Watson, J.B.R., Rosalie (1920). "Conditioned emotional reactions." <u>Journal of Experimental Psychology</u> **3** (1):1-14.

NEUROSEGMENTATION: THE BRAIN OF MEN AND WOMEN

IS OUR BRAIN DIFFERENT?

Women and men are not the same - obviously, we have the same rights and a series of elementary questions about equality that I strongly defend - but biologically, we are not identical. Our physiology differs, our biological objectives, as discussed in previous chapters, are completely distinct, and hence, the focus of importance for this book: our brains are also dissimilar.

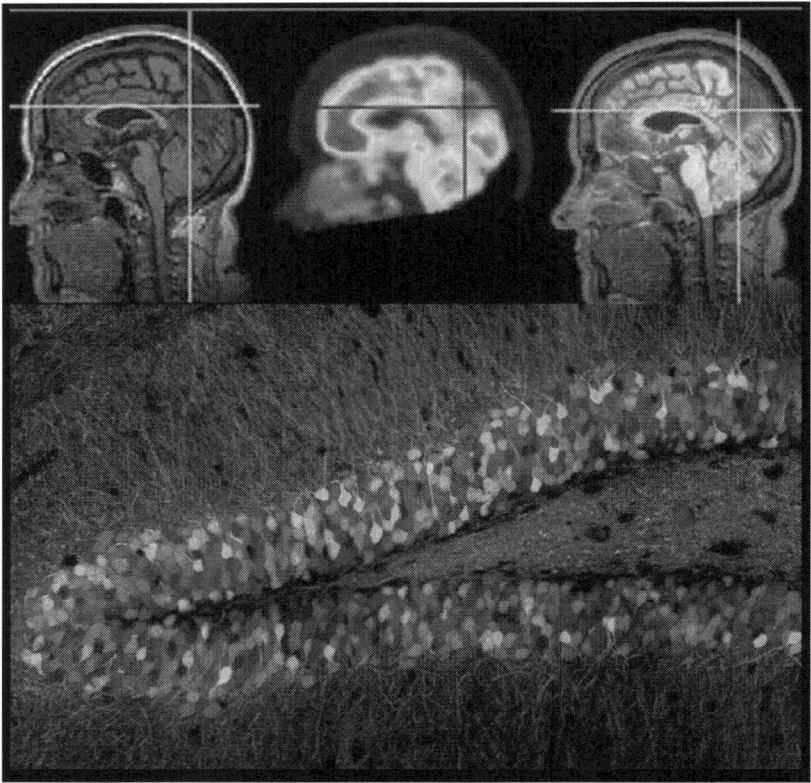

Modern neuroimaging techniques have facilitated the study of anatomical differences between men and women. Most, if not all, of these differences are likely attributed to sex hormones. In fact, the regions that exhibit the greatest disparities are those with a high concentration of receptors for these sex hormones.

New neuroimaging techniques have provided evidence of anatomical variations in numerous brain regions (Goldstein, 2001). Women tend to have more developed frontal cortex regions, which are responsible for higher cognitive processes. Additionally, certain areas of the limbic system, involved in emotional regulation, are larger in women. On the other hand, men tend to have larger parietal structures responsible for spatial perception, as well as an enlarged amygdala, a brain structure involved in emotion-based learning. These differences are influenced by sex hormones, which shape brain architecture during development. It is not surprising that the regions showing anatomical differences between sexes also contain high concentrations of hormone receptors.

However, the differences extend beyond size. Sandra Witelson's research group conducted an analysis of hundreds of postmortem brains and discovered variations in cell density. Specifically, they found that women have higher cell density in regions associated with language comprehension and processing (located in the temporal lobe) as well as in the auditory cortex (SF Witelson, 2006). These findings align perfectly with the higher average scores achieved by women in verbal fluency tests (Maximiliano Echavarri, 2007).

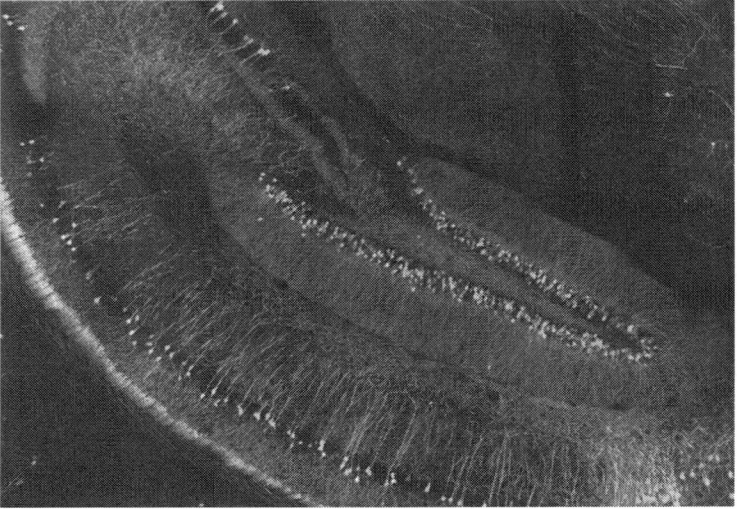

Differences between genders extend beyond variations in the size of specific structures; disparities have also been observed in terms of neuronal density, referring to the number of neurons per square millimeter.

BOTH GENDERS HAVE DIFFERENT PREFERENCES.

Men and women, from an early age, show different preferences. This is evident from personal experience, either with your own children or the children you have observed in your life. Boys and girls choose different toys to play with, and while this is known empirically, there is substantial research supporting it. Boys typically display a clear preference for objects that move, such as balls, bicycles, motorcycles, and cars, while girls show a preference for dolls and activities related to caregiving and family. It is important to note that these observations are based on scientific experiments and not a result of gender bias. The question of whether these differences arise from cultural influences or innate brain disparities has been addressed through well-designed experiments, including studies conducted by Melissa Hines (Hines M 2008). By examining monkeys, which are not subject to cultural influences, it was observed that male monkeys, like their human counterparts, exhibited a preference for "male" toys, while female monkeys preferred "female" toys. This demonstrates that the male gender, in both monkeys and humans, naturally gravitates towards games involving movement, competition, and excitement, which foster skills relevant to their potential roles as males (e.g., hunting, mate selection). Conversely, females tend to select games that develop skills associated with nurturing their offspring. As neuroscientists, we acknowledge that these topics generate debates in society, but it is important to emphasize that these conclusions are drawn from scientific experiments with clear methodologies. We are not the same; we possess distinct internal programming. While cultural factors can influence these preferences, certain inherent differences remain. For example, even with the best intentions, a man will not interpret emotions in the same way as a woman, just as women may not possess the same spatial orientation abilities that men typically exhibit.

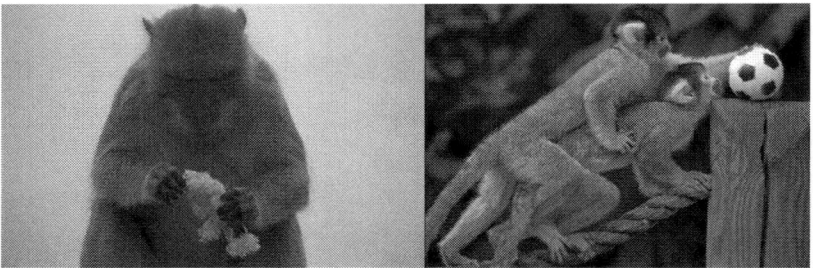

The different preferences observed when choosing toys are innate and not influenced by the environment. These preferences can be observed not only in humans but also in other primates.

WOMEN ARE OFTEN PORTRAYED AS GETTING BORED WITH TECHNOLOGY.

B aron-Cohen and his group (Connellan, 2000) found that young girls spend much more time than boys their age looking at their mothers. These researchers conducted experiments where young children of different sexes watched movies featuring faces and cars, and the results showed that girls paid more attention to faces while boys paid more attention to cars. Furthermore, in a maternity ward, they observed the behavior of one-day-old babies and found that male babies paid more attention to mobile phones while female babies paid more attention to human faces. These findings suggest that we are born with innate preferences. There are numerous studies highlighting these differences, and it should now be clear that we are indeed different. Therefore, it is important to consider these differences in our approach and attention towards both genders. Understanding the target audience and the buyer is crucial, even in the world of perfumery where women are still the primary purchasers, even if it is also for their husbands or sons. From language processing to spatial orientation and the ability to interpret emotional cues, these differences exist. After reading this, do you still have any doubts about women being less attracted to technology than men?

Practical advice:

As we have seen, women generally tend to shy away from technological complexities. It's clear that their brains exhibit this behavior, and we have observed it as early as in babies (Connellan, 2000). Therefore, if your job is to sell technology to a client, you should refrain from focusing on technical specifications and instead engage in a comprehensive educational exercise that highlights the benefits that the technology will bring. Present the advantages in a simple manner and avoid getting caught up in technical details. This advice applies to both genders, but with women, you need to put in extra effort. It is crucial to be careful and ensure that the person in front of you does not feel ignorant. In summary, unless they specifically request technical information, focus on the benefits of your product or service.

Furthermore, it is essential to consider that women's physiology is clearly influenced by cyclical hormonal changes. This means that women may feel completely different today compared to next week. Interpreting their emotions is crucial in order to provide solutions that are better aligned with their actual needs.

GREATER VERBAL FLUENCY IN WOMEN

What is verbal fluency? Psychologist Oscar Castillero defines it exquisitely as "the ability to establish clear and spontaneous dialogue, connecting phrases and ideas naturally and effortlessly, resulting in a continuous and prolonged discourse over time. Fluent speech enables the transmission of ideas and information in an understandable manner, with a suitable rhythm and avoiding unnecessary pauses and disruptions that may hinder comprehension" (Mimenza).

Now, gentlemen, I regret to inform you that, on average, we have less verbal fluency than women, which means that we may have a harder time making ourselves understood within the same timeframe. This is something that you may have observed empirically, but science has also confirmed it (MAXIMILIANO ECHAVARRI 2007). The brain area responsible for verbal fluency is more developed in women (SF Witelson 2006). What does this mean for sales? If you are a woman selling to a man, you may need to speak a bit more slowly. If you are a man selling to a woman, it is best not to rush, as women tend to be more interested in details than men. If you happen to be a woman who naturally speaks at a fast pace, which is relatively common, and tends to skip vocalizing, I recommend that you make an effort to speak to your prospect as if they don't have a perfect understanding of Spanish, taking it a bit more leisurely.

I would like to take this opportunity to debunk a widespread myth - even found in sales books written by non-specialists - that women are more talkative than men. It is simply not true. Both genders, on average, speak around 16,000 words per day (Mehl MR1 2007).

WE DON'T LOOK AT THE SAME SITES.

The interests of women and men differ, and this is also reflected in the websites they visit and the areas they focus on when viewing advertisements. It is crucial to consider this distinction when designing an ad targeted towards a specific gender. When creating an advertisement that includes visual elements, it is advisable to seek guidance from a professional who conducts eye-tracking studies to assess the impact of your advertisement on the intended gender.

WOMEN READ EMOTIONS BETTER THAN MEN.

Y ou can establish a stronger connection with women through emotions, there's no doubt about it. We all know this from personal experience. For instance, observe any family situation when a son arrives with a problem: the father often takes notice only if the matter is serious, while the mother immediately asks, "What's up? What's wrong?" On one hand, we have seen that the limbic system, which manages emotions, is more developed in women (Goldstein 2001). On the other hand, it has been scientifically proven multiple times that emotional reactions are indeed more intense in women. For example, in the ethics section, you can find an experiment conducted by Tania Singer's group. Subjects underwent functional magnetic resonance imaging to monitor their brain activity while watching videos featuring players who cheated and players who respected the rules. Subsequently, all the players received electric shocks. When the non-cheating players received the electric shock, the volunteers who observed these incidents showed activation of regions related to pain through mirror neurons. Women displayed much more intense activation of these regions compared to men, indicating their higher levels of empathy (McCall C 2015). Therefore, it's important to engage the emotional aspect of your potential consumers as much as possible. As a practical tip, keep in mind that connecting with men may require more effort compared to connecting with women.

FASHION FOR MEN AND FASHION FOR WOMEN.

I appreciate the clear approach taken by Inditex regarding the importance of providing differential treatment to men and women. An employee from the group explains it as follows: "In the men's section, the order is strict: sportswear comes first, followed by clothing. The clothes are also organized by matching colors, with the shirt, for example, placed together with the corresponding pants, as men prefer a more coordinated look (...). The space dedicated to women presents a different aspect. Women are creative and appreciate having more freedom to mix and match. Therefore, the garments are not separated by color. It is the customer herself who combines them" (Xabier R. Blanco 2015). As a practical tip, whether you have a small clothing store or a larger establishment, it's advisable to follow these guidelines for providing differentiated treatment to both men and women. Your customers, regardless of their gender, will appreciate it.

BIBLIOGRAPHY

Connellan, J., Baron-Cohen, S, Wheelwright, S, Ba'tki, A, & Ahluwalia, J, (2000). "Sex differences in human neonatal social perception. ." Infant Behavior and Development **23** : 113-118.

Goldstein, J., Seidman, LJ, Horton, NJ, Makris, M, Kennedy, DN, Caviness, VS, Faraone, SV, Tsuang, MT. (2001). "Normal sexual dimorphism of the adult human brain assessed by in-vivo magnetic resonance imaging. ." Cerebral Cortex (11): 490-497.

Hines M, AG (2008). "Monkeys, girls, boys and toys: a confirmation Letter regarding "Sex differences in toy preferences: striking parallels between monkeys and humans"." Horm Behav **54** (3):478-479.

L. Cahill (2003). "Sex- and hemisphere-related influences on the neurobiology of emotionally influenced memory." Prog Neuropsychopharmacol Biol Psychiatry **27** (8):1235-1241.

MAXIMILIANO ECHAVARRI, JCG, FABIÁN OLAZ (2007). "GENDER DIFFERENCES IN COGNITIVE SKILLS AND ACADEMIC PERFORMANCE IN COLLEGE STUDENTS" Univ. Psychol. Bogota Colombia) **6** (2):319-329.

McCall C, S.T. (2015). "Facing off with unfair others: introducing proxemic imaging as an implicit measure of approach and avoidance during social interaction." PLOS One **Feb 12;10(2)** .

Mehl MR1, VS, Ramírez-Esparza N, Slatcher RB, Pennebaker JW. (2007). "Are women really more talkative than men?" Science **6** (317(5834)): 82.

Mimenza, OC "Verbal fluency: 12 psychological tricks to

improve it."

S. F. Witelson, H. B. A. D.L.K. (2006). "Intelligence and brain size in 100 postmortembrains: sex, lateralization and age factors." Brain **129** : 386–398.

Xabier R. Blanco, JS (2015). Amancio Ortega, from zero to Zara

NEUROPHYSIOLOGY OF SENSORY MARKETING

Introduction to Neurophysiology. Basic principles of sensory physiology.

BRIEF INTRODUCTION TO NEUROPHYSIOLOGY

The theoretical framework of neuroscience is vast. In 1997, Eric Kandel, a neuroscientist who won the Nobel Prize in Physiology and Medicine in 2000, wrote a book called "Neuroscience and Behavior" spanning 832 pages (commonly referred to as "the Kandel"). Despite his great synthesis, the content was so extensive that in 2001 he released a condensed version called "Principles of Neuroscience" with "only" 504 pages (known as the "Kandelito" in the field). This demonstrates the immense scope of neuroscience, as even an 8-year college degree in the subject would require further condensation. As a neuroscientist, I humbly acknowledge that our current understanding of neuroscience is merely the tip of the iceberg of reality. There is a philosophical limitation at play: the brain trying to comprehend itself... Can you imagine millions of computers attempting to understand their own functioning? That is essentially what we are trying to do with the brain.

Here, I will provide a brief summary to familiarize those without prior knowledge of neuroscience with the foundational concepts discussed in this book.

The nervous system consists of two main types

of cells: neurons and glia. Neurons have traditionally played the predominant role in information processing, but it is important to note that glia, often referred to as the "sleeping giant" of neuroscience, are increasingly recognized for their significance. Nonetheless, for the purpose of canonical neurophysiology, we will focus on neurons. How many neurons do we have?

If we take the world population and multiply it by fifteen, we would obtain approximately one hundred billion; that is the number of neurons that populate our brain. Overwhelming. Among them, it is estimated that there are about ten thousand different types, and probably, this estimate falls short. They all have to join their precise mate in the right place, and they must not be mistaken. Moreover, each one of them joins and communicates with another 10,000 neurons... (Muotri and Gage 2006). This complex and intricate network is the basis that the brain uses to manage information, acquire knowledge, recognize our loved ones, decide whether or not to buy something, and most importantly, to survive.

How do neurons communicate? After all, the communication between neurons underpins the basis of almost everything that happens in the brain, so it is important to know how they do it. Fundamentally, neurons communicate through what are known as chemical synapses. These are junctions between two neurons where the first releases a series of signaling molecules called neurotransmitters (such as dopamine, serotonin, etc.) into the space between them (synaptic cleft). The second neuron is able to read and interpret these signals and act accordingly. Basically, and to simplify, it could be said that the neuron responds either by turning off and interrupting the chain of communication or by turning on and passing the received information to the following neurons, and so on... Neural circuits are made up of groups of thousands and thousands of neurons communicating with each other. If I ask you what your name is, you will tell me your name thanks to the activation of one of those circuits. By the way, the circuit for our name is one of the most consolidated (because we evoke it daily). The more consolidation, the greater the memory, and vice versa.

Around the chemical synapse, there is a constellation of components that regulate, modulate, and refine this communication. To mention some of these components, we will talk about neuropeptides, which differ from neurotransmitters (for example, endorphins, misnamed "neurotransmitters" in some Neuromarketing books).

Each of the emotions we feel is produced by a cocktail of neurotransmitters. Assigning a single function to a neurotransmitter is a huge mistake, very common among bad popularizers. A neurotransmitter participates in hundreds, thousands of processes, and each of these processes is the result of a certain combination of neurotransmitters. What is true is that, in some processes, one of them clearly predominates. For example, talking about happiness is basically talking about serotonin, talking about dopamine is reward, histamine is sleep... but in these three processes, there are many more neurotransmitters involved, and those three neurotransmitters are involved in many other physiological contexts.

It is important that you know that these circuits and

these cocktails can be manipulated, either from the point of view of emotions, meaning that through a strategy, you can provoke an emotion (which is the result of this cocktail of neurotransmitters) or from a chemical point of view, in such a way that the messenger acts for a longer time (this, for example, is achieved by cocaine or Prozac). Understanding all the components involved in these processes and their mechanism of action is essential to be able to understand and act on the development of information management and decision making.

BASIC PRINCIPLES OF SENSORY PHYSIOLOGY

I f you want to interact with another person, you will inevitably have to do it through one of their senses. There is no other way. Take a moment to think about it. Imagine you are facing a person who cannot see... or hear... or smell... or taste food... or feel through their skin... How would we communicate with them? Impossible. Now, consider that as a salesperson, you generally have the opportunity to interact with your customers through all their senses, and that is something you should take full advantage of. Therefore, it's better for you to learn a little about how the senses work because it is the first step, and an essential one, to "enter" the consumer's brain. Shall we proceed?

To keep the text simple, let's briefly review the classical meanings, although from a physiological perspective, it is infinitely more complex.

First and foremost, Sensory Physiology is based on a relatively simple concept, which is the sensory receptor. Regardless of the sense we are discussing, all senses have sensory receptors that translate and interpret reality for the brain to comprehend. Each receptor is specialized in detecting a specific type of energy and translating it into an electrical language that the brain can understand. What types of sensory receptors exist?

1. Phonoreceptors: Specialized in capturing variations in air pressure, which we generally refer to as hearing (sounds, language, music).
2. Photoreceptors: Specialized in perceiving electromagnetic waves, specifically light. In humans, this translates to vision (images, videos).
3. Chemoreceptors: Specialized in detecting the presence and identity of chemical compounds. The well-known senses in this category are taste (perception of chemical compounds through taste buds) and smell (perception of chemical compounds in the olfactory epithelium). However, chemoreceptors are also found in other parts of the body.
4. Mechanoreceptors: Capable of detecting mechanical deformations, primarily in the skin. This is commonly referred to as the sense of touch (perception of textures, pressure, vibration). It's worth noting that phonoreceptors are a type of mechanoreceptors, but this is mentioned out of curiosity.
5. Thermoreception: Perceives variations in temperature.
6. Nocireception: Responsible for detecting pain. When a tissue can suffer or be damaged, nocireceptors are activated, generating pain signals to indicate that something is not right. Nocireceptors exist in all the previously mentioned modalities. For instance, in complete darkness, one may not be aware that a bright light

can cause harm (photoreception), just as a pinch (mechanoreception), a burn (thermoreception), a loud sound (phonoreception), or an acid abrasion (chemoreception).

It's important to understand that the only reality we know is what our senses show us. But do they provide an accurate representation? The answer is actually no. Our senses were not designed to give us a precise perspective of the external world. They sufficiently replicate it for us to survive, but if you test each sense individually, you will discover interesting phenomena. For example, each eye has a blind spot where no retina exists, and therefore, no images can be formed. Similarly, if you place two sticks ten centimeters apart on your back, you will likely feel only one of them... and so on. To add another example: in the "real world," colors do not actually exist. Rather, our brain interprets different wavelengths of light and assigns colors accordingly.

I anticipate that, through language, you can and should engage the senses. It is not the same to describe oranges as "Florida oranges" or "juicy oranges," or to portray sea bass fillets as "succulent sea bass fillets" (Krishna, 2012).

SCENT MARKETING AND SOUND BRANDING

SCENT NEUROMARKETING: THE SMELL OF MONEY.

"Smell is the most fragile sense, and at the same time the most enduring, farthest from the tangible, and the most persistent... It carries, within its almost impalpable essence, the vast structure of a memory".

Marcel Proust (In Search of Lost Time)

Our world, that of human beings, is less and less olfactory, but we come from animals with an extraordinarily developed sense of smell. What's more, the environment of other mammals is much more olfactory than visual. Thanks to their sense of smell, these animals can map their environment with absolute precision, and in tenths of a second compare a detected odor with the thousands of stored "smell files" and the emotions they aroused. And here, as always, if the smell is new it is stored and if it is familiar, all the emotions around that smell are quickly extracted. For example, if a small rodent first detects an odorant X, and what happens immediately after is that it sees a cat that is about to eat it, rest assured that the next time it smells the odorant X it will very realistically evoke the previous situation, although a lot of time has passed since then. We as a species have lost great olfactory capacity, but even so we have a much larger olfactory world than we imagine, and we have not lost the essence of this sense.

Smell, as you can imagine, was not designed to be a perfumer. Originally, that is, when we lived in full contact with nature, it was an excellent sensor and source of learning. Unfortunately only 20% of the fragrances out there smell good, the rest are bearers of bad news, but spotting that bad news is essential for our survival. What is the first thing you do when you have food in the fridge and you suspect that it may be in bad shape ? Indeed, smell it. And you will trust your sense of smell above all things, if your sense of smell gives you bad news, you will discard it immediately. It is true that if it passes the smell test then you will try it with caution, savoring the food through the taste buds and you will only decide to swallow it if it passes that second control. And you will do the same if you land on a deserted island and come across a food that you have never seen, the first thing you will do is smell it. Therefore, as you can see, smell is essential for survival (WHITE 2015) (Mark F. Bear 2016) .

This sense is one of the most special, without any doubt. The rest of the senses undergo a more or less elaborate processing before reaching the emotional part of the brain, however smell goes directly... with hardly any processing, which is why an iron, timeless association is produced between the odorant that it smells and the emotion that the situation in which it smells arouses. Smelling play dough can instantly transport you to your preschool classroom. Smelling a perfume can evoke a person with astonishing clarity and so with everything... We have very little room for maneuver to influence, from a rational point of view, the emotions that an aroma arouses in us. How could the world of Marketing not take advantage of the sublime virtues of this sense?

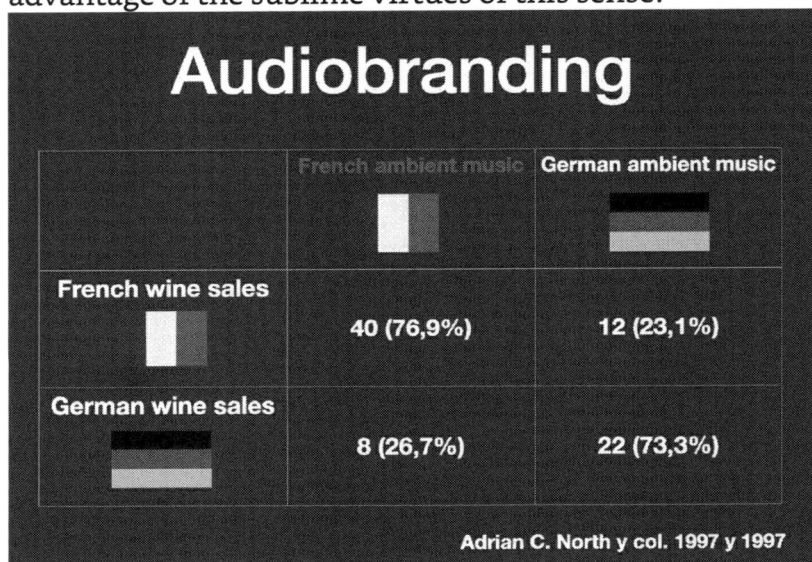

Audiobranding

	French ambient music	German ambient music
French wine sales	40 (76,9%)	12 (23,1%)
German wine sales	8 (26,7%)	22 (73,3%)

Adrian C. North y col. 1997 y 1997

The neuroscientist Gemma Calvert found that the combination of image plus fragrance is much more powerful than both alone (Lindstrom 2012) . He also discovered something surprising, and that is that when we associate a smell with a brand, the same visual regions in the brain are activated that would be activated when seeing the product (Lindstrom 2012) . A very illustrative example is smelling freshly made coffee and imagining the cup of coffee.

Martin Lindstrom, one of the marketing gurus and author of the book Buyology (Lindstrom 2012) , claims that the smell of freshly made hamburgers in fast food restaurants comes from an artificial odorant marketed under the name RTX9338PIS and distributed through ducts. of ventilation. Personally I have been trying to find reliable information about it and I have found absolutely nothing, so I keep this information in quarantine, although I think it is important that you know of its existence. What I do attest to is that it is marketed with the aroma of freshly baked bread (you can find it at https://www.centhylon.com/) . The smell of freshly baked bread, as we will see in the "Neuromarketing in the Shopping Center" section, stimulates appetite at the central nervous system level and increases purchases.

Practical tips:

- *If you are responsible for a food establishment, whether it's a neighborhood store or a large commercial area, using artificial fragrance of freshly baked bread will boost your sales.*
- *If you own a café, you can also invest in an artificial coffee aroma, especially if your café is located in a shopping center, as it will also increase your sales.*

Olfactory marketing, or scent marketing, can be much more sophisticated, as demonstrated by an interesting experiment conducted by Dunkin' Donuts (see the corresponding video in the supplementary material of the book at www.jonathanbenitosipos.com; the access key is 2356). What they did was install a series of scent diffusers with an artificial coffee fragrance on buses. These scent diffusers were activated exclusively when the Dunkin' Donuts jingle played. At bus stops, there were advertisements for the company, and at the end of the journey, there was a Dunkin' Donuts establishment. Through this type of advertising, sales at the establishment increased by 16%.

In Spain, there is a company that is excelling in this

practice, and it is the retail chain "El Ganso". They have designed a very pleasant exclusive fragrance that has become the brand's identity. Wherever you smell it, you immediately associate it with the fashion that the brand offers. It has a significant impact on brand identity and also serves as a great attraction for customers. I have personally witnessed customers in a shopping center who have caught a whiff of the fragrance (as it emanates from the store) and started looking for the store. Once you have the customer in the store, you have already made significant progress.

Therefore, companies are dedicating more and more resources to developing their own signature scents, and they are enjoying the numerous benefits of this practice, which also greatly enhances the shopping experience and positively impacts customer satisfaction with the brand.

THE IMPORTANCE OF MUSIC IN SALES: SOUND BRANDING

M ore than twenty years ago, neuroscientists demonstrated how background music in a supermarket can influence consumer behavior. Researchers from the University of Leicester in England conducted one of the most interesting experiments in this regard. They displayed four French wines and four German wines in the beverage section of a supermarket, arranging them on four shelves with each shelf containing a French and a German wine, along with their respective national flags. To avoid bias, the arrangement of the wines was reversed halfway through the experiment (North 1999) (Adrian C. North 1997). The background music alternated, with typical French music playing on one day and popular German music playing on the next. The results were surprising:

As seen in the table, on the day that French music played, the sale of French wines significantly surpassed that of German wines, and vice versa when German music played.

Were consumers aware that the music was influencing their purchase decisions? Not at all. A survey was conducted explicitly asking them if the music had influenced their choices, and they were completely unaware of its influence. This experiment draws many conclusions, but the main message is clear: music can act on the subconscious and significantly influence the decisions we make.

Therefore, it is important to carefully select the music that plays in our establishments. Piped classical music, for example, has been shown to help reduce vandalism. In fact, during 2006, speakers in the London Underground played classical music, resulting in a 33% decrease in theft (Lindstrom 2012). There are also findings regarding music and food consumption. It seems that for food and drink sales to increase, the music should have two components: low volume and a soft rhythm.

Music also has a notable effect on how people move within a given establishment. Songs with a cadence of 72 beats per minute have been shown to induce relaxation and, as a result, make us spend more time in the establishment in question (Pontes 2015). As mentioned in the "Neuromarketing in the Shopping Center" section, this is a widely used strategy by large supermarket chains.

Similar to how scents evoke vivid moments and scenes, listening to a specific melody has the ability to intensely evoke memories. Melodies subtly reach the subconscious and have a profound impact there. Companies are starting to recognize this and are investing more resources in what is known as Audiobranding or Sound Branding, which involves associating a specific melody with a brand. The goal is to reinforce the brand identity. Take the case of BBVA, for example, you are likely able to recall their famous melody in which they cleverly incorporated the phrase "go ahead." In this case, the melody was specifically composed by Xabier San Martín, a member of "La Oreja de Van Gogh." Audiobranding enhances the brand's personality and significantly aids in its memorability. When images and sound are presented together, brand perception is more favorable compared to when they are presented separately (Lindstrom 2012). Building a melody is, of course, the work of a musician, and I strongly recommend it. It is now the realm of Neuromarketing to test how effective a particular melody is in the consumer's mind.

Companies are increasingly making efforts to associate their brand with distinctive auditory cues.

But don't underestimate it... audiobranding goes even further. You wouldn't imagine the effort Kellogg's has put into creating a unique and recognizable sound when chewing its cereals, distinguishing them from any other cereal. The same applies to other cookie and chip manufacturers (Lindstrom 2012). Even the sound produced when opening a package of Pringles crisps is deliberately designed and patented! So, never underestimate the power of sounds, and remember, they will become increasingly significant in the future.

NEUROMARKETING OF COLORS AND SOMATOSENSORY NEUROMARKETING

Color Marketing. Nothing can be left to chance.

Each color arouses emotions within us, whether we are aware of it or not.

As previously mentioned, colors do not exist in nature but rather are the brain's interpretation of different wavelengths of light, which behave as waves. Each color evokes emotions, without a doubt. Entering a white room is not the same as entering a red room because the brain interprets the color and triggers an emotion. While not all colors evoke the same emotions in everyone, there are some principles that are nearly pan-cultural or at least practically universal, with some nuances specific to the East/West dichotomy.

If you don't have a budget to hire a Neuromarketing specialist for guidance, here is a comprehensive description (based on scientific studies) of the emotions associated with each color. It's important to be aware of these emotions and exercise caution when combining colors. Pay close attention to different tones as well because within a specific color, different Pantone ranges can convey entirely different meanings to the brain.

I recommend using this information for branding or rebranding purposes, such as decorating your premises, designing packaging, bags, the website, or even your logo. Nothing should be left to chance... each color unconsciously communicates something, so make the most of it for your own benefit. Let's get started!

White

It is a color that represents purity, sincerity, and happiness (Aslam 2006, Labrecque 2011). It is associated with cleanliness, freshness, simplicity, and minimalism.

A commercial example is Apple, which has extensively used the color white, representing the mentioned emotions.

The Apple company has known how to effectively utilize the qualities of white for many years to emphasize minimalism and, in turn, the sophistication of its products.

Yellow

Traditionally, yellow is associated with sunlight, joy, and enthusiasm. It conveys happiness, energy, fun, spontaneity, joy, innovation, competence, and ability (Aslam 2006, Labrecque 2011). However, it's important to be cautious as research suggests that yellow is one of the most ambiguous colors. At times, it can also represent anger, envy, and betrayal. Therefore, when using yellow, it must be approached with care. Overloading with yellow can potentially lead to irritation in the observer.

Commercial examples: IKEA, Mc Donald's

Ikea opted for yellow (mixed with blue, likely inspired by the Swedish flag) from the beginning, conveying energy, innovation, and spontaneity.

Red

It conveys power, desire, lust, arousal, and love (Aslam 2006, Labrecque 2011, Piotrowski 2012). It is perhaps the most extensively studied color and yields the highest consensus in research results. It is commonly associated with passion, strength, revolution, impulsiveness, virility, and danger. Undoubtedly, some of these associations are related to the fact that blood is red. Wearing red encourages us to behave in a slightly more assertive and outgoing manner.

Clearly, the color red is predominant in most fast food establishments. Some authors suggest that it enhances sensory perception of food and motivates greater consumption.

Studies also conclude that the color red increases heart rate and triggers an adrenaline rush. Consequently, individuals observing red become more energetic.

Commercial examples: Red boxes of chocolates, fast food outlets, Ferrari, Coca-Cola.

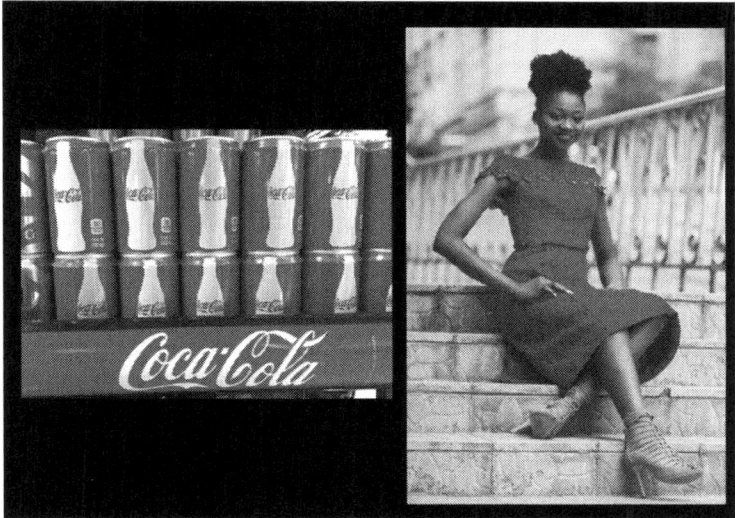

The passion, strength, and impulsiveness conveyed by red are unquestionable. Undoubtedly, the fact that blood is red has a lot to do with it.

Orange

It is a color associated with enthusiasm, action, lust, sensuality, and exaltation. It is one of the colors that have been less studied.Commercial examples: Fanta, Amazon.

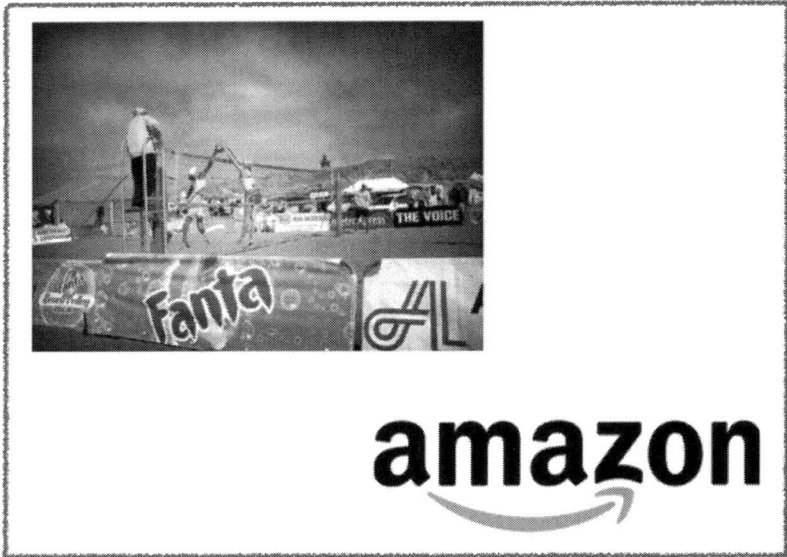

Orange is one of the colors that have received less research attention. Fanta has been using it as a reference color since its inception, probably to reinforce the association with the fruit. The case of Amazon deserves a slightly more detailed explanation. Its logo is loaded with symbolism—the arrow takes you from A to Z, implying that you can find everything you need. At the same time, it forms a smile, which is unlikely to go unnoticed by the subconscious. It conveys proximity and trust.

Blue

It is a color that conveys competence, masculinity, high quality, and is often used as a corporate color (Aslam 2006, Labrecque 2011). It is associated with the color of the sky and water, representing tranquility and freshness. Blue is an elegant and commonly used color in the business world.

Commercial examples: Facebook or Twitter.

Here are three examples of large companies that use blue as their corporate color. It is interesting to note how each company utilizes different shades of blue, giving them distinct personalities.

Green

Green evokes youth, a love of nature, and good taste; although it is also associated with envy (Aslam 2006). It is a color that conveys youthfulness and hope. There is growing evidence that a room painted green promotes relaxation.

Green is widely used in "eco and bio" products that are currently popular, often combined with recycled cardboard packaging.

Commercial examples: Starbucks, Garnier (emphasizing the naturalness of their shampoos).

It is no coincidence that green is the color of chlorophyll, which in turn gives leaves their green hue. The brain interprets green as the color of nature and the peace that surrounds it.

Purple

It is a color that evokes luxury, quality, royalty, sophistication, authority, and power (Aslam 2006, Labrecque 2011). In ancient Rome, it was a color completely forbidden for the common people due to the law of Tyrian purple.

Commercial examples: Cadbury, Yahoo, Milka, Cabify.

In the past, purple was obtained from the mollusk *Murex brandaris* through a complex and laborious process. It took 12,000 shells to obtain just 1.4 grams of pure dye, making its price more expensive than gold. The Romans considered this color to be imposing, and its use was prohibited among the common people. Indeed, it conveys elegance, luxury, and power. Here, we can see one example of company that use this color

Pink

Pink is a color that evokes sincerity, sophistication, femininity, sweetness, sensuality, exquisiteness, and delicacy (Aslam 2006, Labrecque 2011). Some bright shades are directly associated with sexual connotations.

Business examples that utilize the color include Hello Kitty and Victoria's Secret.

Pink

VICTORIA'S
SECRET

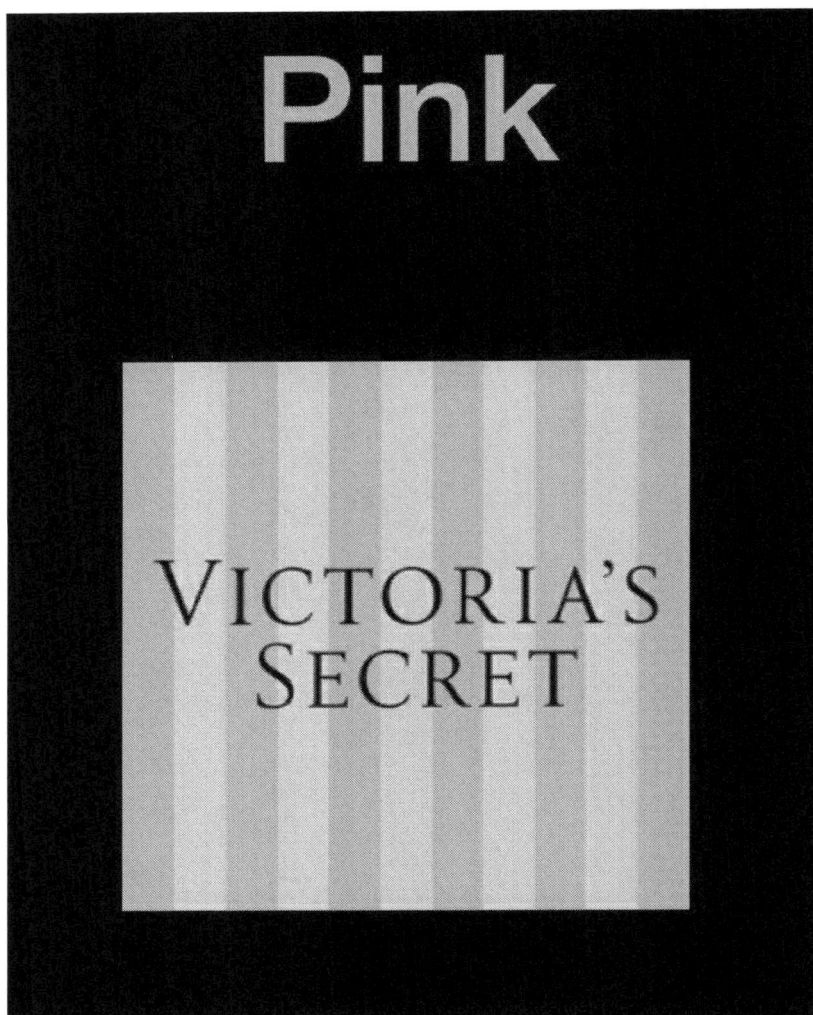

Undoubtedly, pink conveys a sense of delicacy. Victoria's Secret
maximizes this delicacy and sensuality, which are the hallmarks

216

of its brand.

Black

Black transmits sophistication, glamour (which is accentuated when combined with gold), exclusivity, seriousness, sorrow, and fear.

Commercial examples of brands associated with black include Chanel and Hugo Boss.

Commercial examples that mix black with gold include Lamborghini.

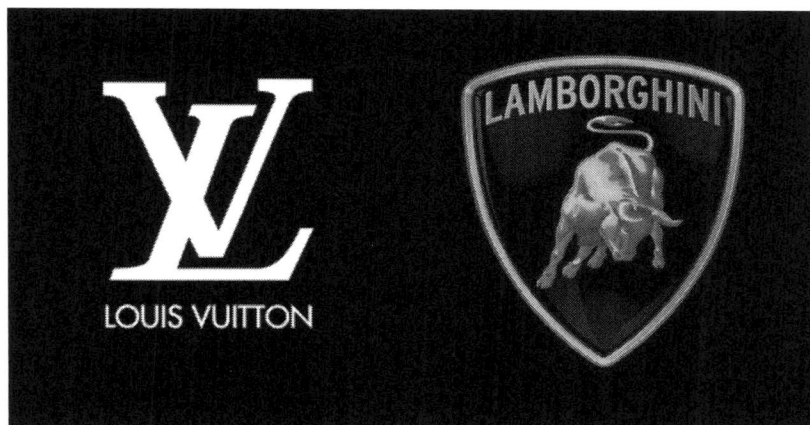

The color black already conveys a sense of sophistication and glamour, but it intensifies even more when combined with gold.

Brown

t is a color that conveys warmth, reliability, security, confidence, and sometimes even harshness (Labrecque

2011).

Business Example: UPS

The color brown conveys security and confidence. In addition to UPS, one can also think about the color of Prosegur suits

Black and white

Black and white images are often associated with elegance and evoke a sense of truthfulness. However, certain precautions must be taken as they can also convey nostalgia and even pessimism.

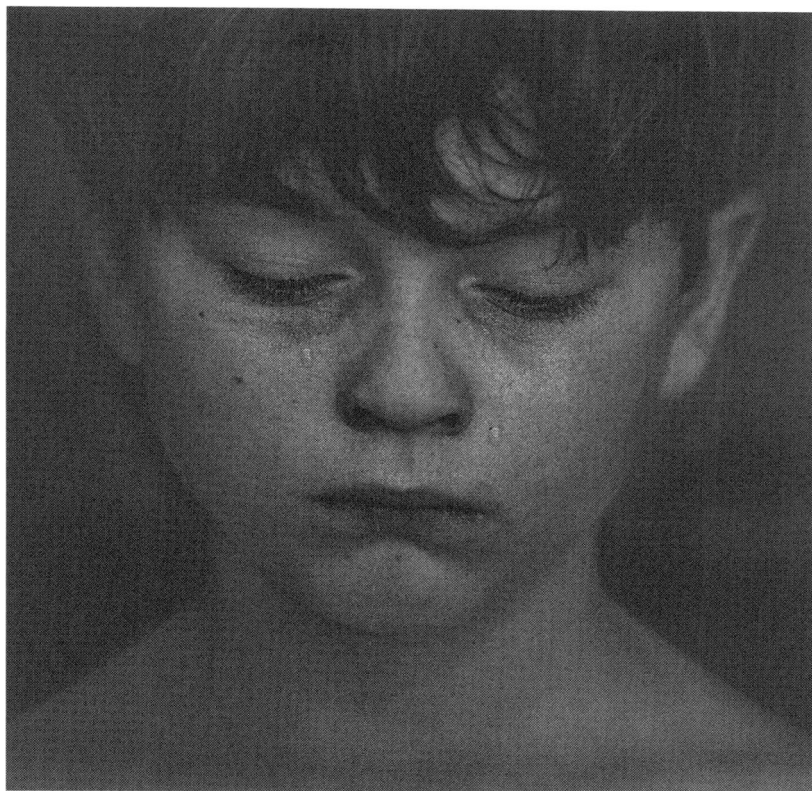

Black and white images convey both elegance and veracity.

SOMATOSENSORY NEUROMARKETING (TOUCH MARKETING)

Perhaps you have never consciously thought about it, but since infancy, our world relies much more on the sense of touch than we realize. Touch becomes useful to us even inside the womb. At just 8 weeks of gestation, the human embryo is capable of responding to contact with the cheek (Krishna, 2012). By 26 weeks, the embryo can grasp anything that falls into its hand, including the umbilical cord (Krishna, 2012). Surprisingly, experiments with macaque monkeys have shown that newborns prefer a cloth dummy that cannot nurse over a wire dummy that can (refer to figure) (Harlow, 1958). These findings emphasize the significance of touch (texture) in your products.

We, as animals, have a strong reliance on the sense of touch, and this dependence begins in the womb. The experiments with monkeys, where they choose a false mother made of artificial skin over a metallic mother that provides nourishment, further confirm our reliance on this sense. You can personally experience the need for touch when encountering new products in any shopping center.

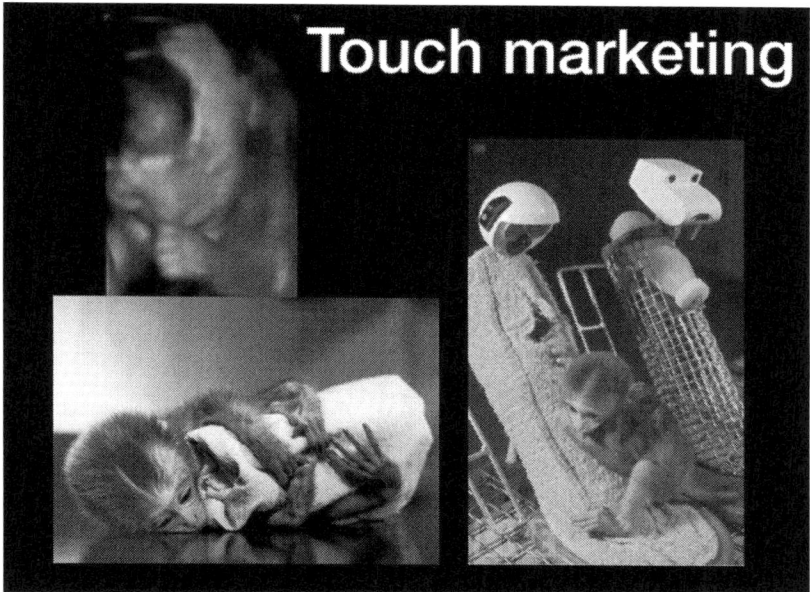

Touch marketing

We, as animals, have a strong reliance on the sense of touch, and this dependence begins in the womb. The experiments with monkeys, where they choose a false mother made of artificial skin over a metallic mother that provides nourishment, further confirm our reliance on this sense. You can personally experience the need for touch when encountering new products in any shopping center.

We have a natural inclination to touch everything, and if you haven't noticed, just think about visiting a shopping center where you encounter various products, such as clothing or technology. Have you ever realized how strong the urge is to touch everything? As you can imagine, the information obtained through this sense, known as somatosensory in Physiology, evokes specific emotions within us. These emotions, in the complex pathways of our brain, can transform into desires to possess the object, influencing our desire to buy.

The somatosensory system consists of several sensory divisions, and the ones that have the most impact when evaluating a product are: (Mark F. Bear 2016) (WHITE 2015):

- Mechanoreception: This division is responsible for interpreting mechanical deformations that occur on the skin, such as the sensation of passing your fingertips through a soft layer of velvet. Pleasant textures have a significant influence, and I encourage companies to make an effort (as some have been doing for years) to ensure their products leave a pleasant somatosensory impression. Consider the difference between touching a rough-textured object and a smooth, rubbery-textured one.
- Thermoreception: This ability allows us to detect different temperatures. For certain products, it is essential that the thermal sensation transmitted by an object feels warm rather than cold. Materials that conduct temperature poorly, like synthetic polymers or plastics, can propagate a greater sensation of warmth compared to materials that conduct temperature very well, such as metals.

The perception of weight is equally significant. A heavy object does not provide the same sense of robustness as a lighter one. Manufacturers are aware of this and sometimes deliberately add weight to objects to enhance the feeling of solidity. For instance, Bang & Olufsen does this with some of its remote controls by incorporating additional metallic filling, giving them a more robust appearance and, in a way, justifying their price (Lindstrom 2012).

A combination of all these sensations is exemplified by the experience of unpacking an Apple iPhone. The choice of materials is not arbitrary; it involves durable cardboard with a plastic protective layer that enhances the tactile pleasure. The precise fit of the two components is not accidental either. Anyone who has opened that box remembers the sensation, which is achieved through a small suction effect between the pieces. It creates a pleasant experience that inevitably shapes your opinion about the product, and it is just one of the numerous patents held by Apple (KAHNEY 2009).

Anyone who has opened an iPhone case for the first time has likely experienced a series of distinct and delightful sensations that are etched into their memory forever. The patented box in which they are sold enhances the overall experience and strongly reinforces the perception of sophistication and product quality.

L'Oréal designed an advertising campaign focused on the sense of touch in the United Kingdom. It featured a double-page print advertisement. The first page had a rough texture, while the second page was smooth. The message conveyed was clear and impactful: the treatment leaves your skin silky and wrinkle-free (Izquierdo 2013). This case exemplifies a tactile mini-drama, which, as we see in various instances throughout the book, is well understood by our brains.

Similarly, the beer brand Heineken has incorporated intriguing tactile elements in both their bottles and cans. The bottles feature relief, including tactile interactions such as embossed letters, enhancing the drinking experience. The cans take it a step further with the use of ink formed by embossed microdots, providing a palpable sensation that is distinctive (Izquierdo 2013).

It is evident that the industry should pay more attention to the sense of touch, both in the design and marketing of new products.

practical advice

Consider how you can enhance the tactile perception of your product. Does it need to be lighter? Heavier to convey a sense of robustness? Are the materials pleasant to the touch? If you have limited options to modify the product itself, focus on improving its packaging. Well-designed packaging can significantly increase its symbolic value and, consequently, boost sales. The size of the packaging also influences customers' perception of value and visibility on the shelf. Additionally, if the packaging can serve a future purpose, it adds even more value. For example, toiletry bags in the perfume industry or boxes that transform into cans or desk organizers with the brand logo, among others.

BIBLIOGRAPHY

Aslam, MM (2006). "Are You Selling the Right Colour? A Cross-cultural Review of Color as a Marketing Cue." Journal of Marketing Communications **12** (1):15-30.

Bear MF, CBW, Paradiso MA (2009). Neuroscience. Exploring the brain., Masson Ed.

Harlow, H.F. (1958). "The nature of love." American Psychologist **13** (12): 673-685.

Left, PBR (2013). Your money and your brain: Why we make wrong decisions and how to avoid them according to neuroeconomics, Conecta.

KAHNEY, L. (2009). Steve Jobs Awarded Patent For iPhone Packaging. Cult of Mac.

Krishna, A. (2012). "An integrative review of sensory marketing: Engaging the senses to affect perception, judgment and behavior." Journal of Consumer Psychology **22** 332–351.

Labrecque, LIM, GR (2011). "Exciting red and competent blue: the importance of color in marketing." Journal of the Academy of Marketing Science **40** (5):711-727.

Lindstrom, M. (2012). Buyology. Truths And Lies Of Why We Buy - 1st Edition, Booket. Divulgation. Present.

Piotrowski, CA, T (2012). "Color Red: Implications for applied psychology and marketing research." Psychology and Education: an Interdisciplinary Journal. **49** (1):55-57.

NEUROMARKETING IN A SHOPPING CENTER

A t this point in the book, you can envision the display of neuromarketing techniques that can be found in a shopping center. Nothing is left to chance; everything is meticulously studied to ensure that we leave with more products than we actually need. Whether you are responsible for a large commercial area or a modest establishment, there are several key aspects to consider:

Anti-clockwise direction

Firstly, the entrance is positioned to the right of the checkouts, and this is not by chance. It almost compels customers to navigate through the store counterclockwise, which has been shown to increase sales by 10% (Pontes 2015). There is a reason behind this phenomenon. Have you ever noticed which way runners typically go on a track? They run counterclockwise, just like the supermarket layout encourages. Furthermore, if a person closes their eyes and tries to walk straight, they will naturally drift to the left. The majority of people are right-handed, and even left-handed individuals tend to be right-legged, making counterclockwise movement more comfortable. Feeling comfortable allows us to pay more attention to our surroundings, thereby increasing the likelihood of making a purchase.

How we navigate the aisles

Interestingly, as consumers, we typically prefer to enter through the ends of the aisles and exit where we entered, covering the entire length. As a result, products in the middle of the aisles receive less attention than those at the ends (Jeffrey S. Larson 2005). It is also effective to place familiar brands at the beginning of the aisle as they serve as a welcoming presence and encourage customers to explore further (Jeffrey S. Larson

2005).

In large supermarkets, they facilitate counterclockwise movement for us. Due to right leg dominance, we find it easier to turn left than right, which creates a more comfortable experience and allows us to pay greater attention to our surroundings.

Advice:
Consider designing strategies in your establishment to

guide customers in an anti-clockwise direction, particularly in areas that you want their attention focused on. If you have aisles, place well-known products at the beginning of the aisle. Avoid placing important products in the middle of the aisles. In the checkout area, position "one shot" or impulse products (low-priced items that are typically not premeditated purchases and are decided upon seeing them on display, often in towers or dumps).

Other factors to consider include the height at which products are placed. Items you want to sell should be at eye level for maximum visibility. Differentiating labels, special signage (such as stoppers), stands, or glorifiers can enhance product visibility. Essential products (such as oil, flour, sugar, salt, etc.) can be relocated once or twice a year to encourage customers to explore different areas of the store.

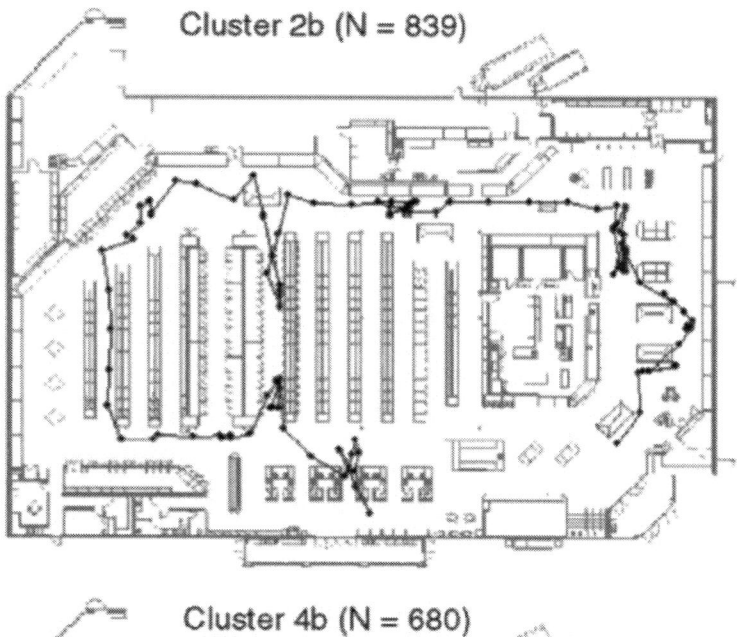

Cluster 2b (N = 839)

Cluster 4b (N = 680)

The studies conducted indicate that we typically do not walk through the aisles from start to finish. Instead, we enter through one end, walk a little, and exit through the same end. Therefore, it is not advisable to place products of interest for sale in the middle of the aisle.

Cafeteria at the entrance

Have you noticed that more and more large supermarkets have recently installed a cafeteria at the entrance? Why is that? For a simple reason: to unconsciously stimulate our hunger. They don't necessarily expect you to make a purchase there, although it's a bonus if you do. The main objective of this strategy is to encourage us to buy more when we go grocery shopping hungry. That's why one of the common advice given to consumers is to never go shopping on an empty stomach. In the Sensory Marketing section, I suggest that if you have a food establishment and don't have enough space for a bread oven, you can use an artificial scent that smells like freshly baked bread.

The cafeteria also serves two additional purposes. Firstly, it provides a comfortable place where a companion can wait, as typically men dislike shopping and women tend to increase their average shopping basket when they are not under the pressure of their partners. Secondly, if the shopping trip is taking too long and you feel tempted to give up, you can take a break at the cafeteria and then continue.

Another strategy employed by some large supermarket chains is placing the cafeteria right in the center of the hypermarket, complete with product tastings and chairs to sit on. They have the bread oven at the entrance to stimulate consumers' appetites, and with the central location of the cafeteria, they aim to prolong the customers' stay in the establishment. And of course, offering free Wi-Fi.

Distribution of certain products

As we navigate through the supermarket, it won't be long before we encounter the fruit and vegetable section. This placement is not random but intended to give us the perception that we are in a place where healthy products are sold. Basic necessities are typically positioned at the back of the supermarket, compelling us to navigate through the entire store, thus increasing the chances of adding additional items to our cart. You may also notice deliberate gaps on the shelves to create the impression that other customers have already purchased that product (herd effect), enticing us not to miss out. Cross-selling is also significant in product arrangement, with complementary items placed next to the main product. For example, corkscrews near the higher-priced wine section and nutcrackers with walnuts during the Christmas season.

Background music

As mentioned in the Audiobranding section, music is also part of a deliberate strategy. Songs with a rhythm of 72 beats per minute create a sense of calm and make us spend more time in the supermarket (Pontes 2015).

shopping carts

It is not a coincidence that almost every cart you choose tends to veer in one direction. This maneuver is another tactic employed to boost sales.

Shopping carts are often intentionally unbalanced, with a tendency to veer to one side, in the hope of giving shoppers more opportunities to see items in the aisles and, consequently, make more purchases. However, some shopping centers have taken this approach to an extreme, which ends up irritating customers.

Supply effect

An interesting tactic is to place a large quantity of a specific product in a strategic location. You may have wondered why there are hundreds of cans of a particular brand of tuna in the middle of one of the main aisles, relatively far from the other tuna brands. This is clearly a well-studied strategy. Interestingly, one of our brain's heuristic shortcuts is to assume that if a product is displayed in such large quantities, it must be on offer or discounted, leading to a remarkable increase in its sales. In many cases, it is even advertised as a special offer, although it may not necessarily be one. Usually, the supplier has paid extra for this prominent placement.

NEUROMARKETING CODE OF ETHICS

ETHICS OF NEUROMARKETING

" With a lie, you can go very far, but without the possibility of returning".
jewish proverb

This chapter is intentionally short and concise because I believe its content is crucial, and I want to avoid repetitive rhetoric that may cause you to lose focus.

Neuromarketing has been a subject of controversy since its inception, mainly due to its potential for abuse. The lack of understanding about this science and its scope has led to significant concerns within society. Neuromarketing has been viewed as a tool for manipulating consumers' minds, and while it is true that it can be misused in such a manner, it ultimately depends on how it is employed. Science provides knowledge that can be used for both good and bad purposes. For instance, physics has facilitated connecting loved ones through advancements in telecommunications and transportation, but it has also led to the creation of devastating weapons of mass destruction. The ethics of neuromarketing solely depend on how we choose to utilize it. Therefore, it is crucial to establish ethical guidelines for its application. Until there are specific regulations governing neuromarketing, I will share my perspective based on accumulated experience and how I would like you to use the knowledge from this book.

It is essential to prioritize people, particularly consumers, above everything else. I find any exceptions to this principle reprehensible. Neuromarketing should never be used to deceive or instill unnecessary fears or needs. Instead, it should be employed for precisely the opposite purpose. It should be utilized to identify and better understand customers' needs and fears, mitigate those fears, and effectively satisfy their needs. Any other use is contemptible. By aligning products and services with the genuine needs of customers, higher sales can be achieved, along with increased satisfaction and loyalty.

Neuromarketing should establish a win-win relationship where everyone benefits. I emphasize that it must never be used to sell consumers something they don't need. Such behavior is completely reprehensible, and transparency and honesty should always prevail.

When properly utilized, neuromarketing significantly optimizes the resources of companies and, consequently, the planet. Companies can gain accurate insights into how their products and services interact with potential customers even before launching them to the market. Traditional marketing techniques like focus groups and surveys often fail because individuals unconsciously express intentions that differ from their actual behaviors. This leads to resource wastage within companies, which is unfavorable in a world striving for sustainability. To avoid unnecessary expenditure of time and money on focus groups, companies should employ experts, either internally or externally, who can make decisions based on experience and data interpretation quickly and efficiently. They should also conduct rapid tests or studies, often online or within a small group of establishments, before a full-scale rollout. Additionally, it is crucial to keep an eye on competitive initiatives.

A neuromarketing expert should carefully listen to clients, analyze their fears and needs with genuine interest, and create products or services that address those concerns. It is despicable to generate fear and then offer a product as a solution. As I have mentioned throughout the book, honesty is a powerful selling point. Being honest is not only morally right but also beneficial in the medium and long term.

And this concludes our journey through Neuromarketing! I hope you have learned and enjoyed it, and that you can apply the tools we have explored here. If you enjoyed the book, I would greatly appreciate it if you could leave a comment on the Amazon page where you purchased it. Your feedback is incredibly valuable to us.

I wish you the best of luck in the future and hope you achieve great success. By success, I mean that your eyes shine with happiness every day of your life. Good luck! @_jonathanbenito

JONATHAN BENITO SIPOS

Made in the USA
Columbia, SC
19 February 2025